Essential
Kitchens

DESIGN BASICS • BEFORE & AFTER • BASIC SKILLS
EQUIPPING YOUR KITCHEN • MATERIALS & SURFACES

Essential Kitchens

This Old House® Books

EDITORIAL DIRECTOR Paul Spring

Development Team

EDITOR Mark Feirer
ART DIRECTOR Sue Ng
PICTURE EDITOR Susan Sung Danelian
COPY EDITOR Steven H. Saltzman
PRODUCTION COORDINATOR Robert Hardin
PRODUCTION ASSOCIATE Leenda Bonilla

Special thanks to: Anthony Wendling, Anthony Cortazzo, Joseph Milidantri

Time Inc.
HOME ENTERTAINMENT

PRESIDENT Rob Gursha
VICE PRESIDENT, BRANDED BUSINESSES David Arfine
EXECUTIVE DIRECTOR, MARKETING SERVICES Carol Pittard
DIRECTOR, RETAIL & SPECIAL SALES Tom Mifsud
DIRECTOR OF FINANCE Tricia Griffin
MARKETING DIRECTOR Kenneth Maehlum
PRODUCT MANAGER Dennis Sheehan
EDITORIAL OPERATIONS MANAGER John Calvano
ASSOCIATE PRODUCT MANAGER Sara Stumpf
ASSISTANT PRODUCT MANAGER Linda Frisbie

Special thanks to: Suzanne DeBenedetto, Robert Dente, Gina Di Meglio, Peter Harper, Roberta Harris, Natalie McCrea, Jessica McGrath, Jonathan Polsky, Emily Rabin, Mary Jane Rigoroso, Steven Sandonato, Tara Sheehan, Meredith Shelley, Bozena Szwagulinski, Marina Weinstein, Niki Whelan

Published by

This Old House.
BOOKS

Time Publishing Ventures, Inc.
1185 Avenue of the Americas
New York, NY 10036

First Edition
ISBN: 1-929049-54-4
Library of Congress Catalogue Number: 2001095929

We welcome your comments and suggestions about *This Old House* books. Please write to us at:
This Old House Books
Attention: Book Editors
P.O. Box 11016
Des Moines, IA 50336-1016

If you would like to order any of the *This Old House* books, please call us at 1-800-678-2643.

First Edition, ISBN 1-929049-54-4

Contents

INTRODUCTION Remodeling even a modest kitchen isn't easy. Jammed with work surfaces, tool storage, and various large pieces of equipment, it's a room often compared to a workshop. Alas, it isn't nearly that easy to build. A workshop isn't burdened by the often contradictory demands of working well and looking good. A shop also doesn't require daily cleaning to bring it to sanitary standards.

And it needn't manage the combined traffic patterns of a railroad switching station, restaurant, storage depot, conference center, and landing zone. Because we expect so much of our kitchens, much has been written about improving them. However, we hope you'll find this book as different from the crowd of typical titles as you do *This Old House* magazine itself.

This is a how-to guide—but only in the broadest sense of the term. Yes, you'll learn how to choose and install materials, but you'll also discover a lot of new ideas and get to peer over the shoulders of other homeowners and designers as they transform tired old kitchens into dynamic new kitchens. Our aim is not just to inform, but also to inspire and encourage you. That's because we know from experience that there's one task that's harder than learning how to lay out a work triangle, pick out countertops, or hang cabinets: getting started. So let this book serve as your muse, and take the first step towards making your kitchen turn out just the way you want it to.   —*THE EDITORS*

Design

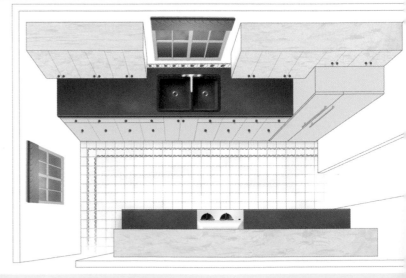

Basics

KEY ISSUES IN PLANNING YOUR KITCHEN REMODEL

ASK ANYONE WHO HAS SURVIVED A KITCHEN REMODEL, AND they'll tell you that it's not a job for the faint of heart. Even if you're not the one stripping paint and pounding nails, the process is often difficult, and more time-consuming than expected. A typical kitchen is filled with expensive equipment and laced with a hidden network of vents, water pipes, and wiring, making it the most complex room in a house. But there is a way to do this work right. For one thing, design and plan it carefully—rush in and your psyche will suffer as much as your checkbook. Get plenty of advice, make up your own mind . . . and then work with professionals you trust.

Keeping Costs Down

If you take time to plan your project, you'll spend less cash to complete it

WHEN NEW YORK CITY ARCHITECT DENNIS Wedlick takes on a renovation project, he often finds himself persuading the client not to spend lavishly on it. "People think that unless they use the most expensive paint or tile or trim, they won't end up with the look they want," he says. "But a high-quality outcome depends on good design, not high-priced materials." Nowhere is that more important than in a kitchen. Over the years, Wedlick has developed a long list of tricks and strategies for keeping budgets in check without compromising the results.

Whenever he can, Wedlick avoids custom-made components such as windows, doors, and cabinets. Standard-size windows cost much less than custom units, he says, yet give up little in looks. To make up for any loss of visual impact that a custom window would provide, Wedlick surrounds the stock unit with unusual trim or simply increases its size. He also clusters stock windows to create a custom effect for a fraction of the custom cost.

Even bigger savings come from choosing stock over custom cabinets (cabinets made exactly to your specifications) that typically cost at least 50 percent more. "What you give up is some variety of size, color, and decorative detail." If stock cabinet lines don't have the features you want, consider moving up to semicustom cabinets—they offer more style, finish, and material choices. They cost more than stock cabinets, to be sure, but are still less expensive than custom cabinets.

In the same way, Wedlick sees no reason to spring for a custom or top-of-the-line door that brings nothing more than a new style to an old opening. He prefers putting a less expensive door into a new location if it will improve the function of a floor plan. Door costs can be further reduced by choosing reasonably priced hardware. "You can spend fifteen hundred dollars on a handle," says Wedlick, "but for around fifty dollars you can get a brushed-chrome doorknob that feels just as expensive."

Elaborate details always cost more, but

RIGHT: When remodeling the kitchen in their 1887 Queen Anne, the owners worked with a team of experienced designers and contractors to keep costs in line. The lesson: Listen to advice, then do what you think is best with people you trust. FAR RIGHT: Ornate molding or a special cabinet to house a nonstandard sink can be expensive.

instead of eliminating them altogether, Wedlick works with simpler, more economical alternatives. In place of fancy crown molding, he often favors plain pine trim—and plenty of it. "The quickest way to make a house look cheap is to skimp on the amount of trim," he warns. "But flat one-by-eight pine boards create a more dramatic frame for a room than a three-inch crown."

Simple detailing can also bring big savings on kitchen counters. You might be able to cut 30 percent from the cost of granite countertops by calling for square edges instead of rounded or beveled edges. And if you're tiling a wall, you can save a lot by eliminating a fancy tile border; try something simple instead, such as a checkerboard pattern made of differing colors of the same tile.

Cost overruns often come from midproject shopping sprees, Wedlick warns, when people go overboard picking out faucets, sinks, and other fixtures. "If you walk into a store and see forty faucets in a row, sure, the one with the elaborate swan's-head spout is going to stand out," he says. "But one with a simple long neck will work just as well." Any triumph of form over function inevitably costs plenty.

Seemingly small expenditures for soap holders, doorway saddles, cabinet door and drawer pulls, and the like can also inflate a budget. "Taken individually, the price difference between a fifty-dollar marble saddle and a ten-dollar tile saddle seems minor," says Susan Goddard, a designer based in Montclair, New Jersey. "But if you bring that attitude to every purchase, you can find yourself thousands of dollars over budget without knowing how you got there." Wedlick has a similar opinion about expensive, elaborate light fixtures—they look beautiful in the showroom but often overpower the room when installed.

Even as Wedlick counsels cost control, though, he encourages his clients to spend more in the right places to raise the quality of a house or reduce maintenance needs. Some upgrades he thinks merit their extra cost: top-quality kitchen appliances, stone countertops, copper water-supply pipes, and lots of electrical outlets.

But a homeowner's best investment, says Wedlick, is to plan the project carefully. That means, in part, interviewing several designers and contractors to make sure you hire the ones who are best able to execute your ideas at reasonable prices. Price out a variety of design and construction options, too; that will minimize major money-consuming changes and mistakes once work begins. "The results of a renovation will last a long time, so the planning needs to be long-term, too," says Wedlick. "The more time you invest up front, the less money you will spend in the end."

Stained-pine cabinets offer a dramatic appearance without an equally dramatic price. This sink may look exotic, but it's just a stainless-steel utility sink with the legs cut off, mounted above a stock cabinet. The backsplash—pine beadboard paneling—is another example of how to use simple materials dramatically.

Consider cost tradeoffs when planning a kitchen. Classic white cabinets are less costly than custom-color cabinets. Here, thermofoil construction (vinyl applied with heat to a core of medium-density fiberboard) reduces cabinet costs further, but extra detailing (and expense) for rope molding, a wine rack, and glazed doors prevents the kitchen from looking plain. The counters are made from solid surfacing, not granite, and the cabinet hardware includes simple knobs.

Design Workbook

Basic kitchen layouts you can use to plan your next project

FOR ALL THE MANY DECISIONS THAT GO INTO COMPLETING a successful kitchen renovation, your most important should also be your first: an ideal layout. No doubt you've heard of the kitchen work triangle—a layout strategy that limits the distance between your sink, stove, and refrigerator. Designers say the total distance of the triangle legs should be no more than 25 feet, but the arrangement can be manipulated in various ways to satisfy your cooking needs. The result should be a convenient and safe kitchen, with plenty of storage just where you need it the most. To help you determine the optimal layout for your kitchen, here are six prototypical floor plans. A variation of one of them is probably the perfect shape for your new kitchen.

ISLAND

When space allows, adding a work island to a kitchen with an L- or U-shape will dramatically improve its function. Instantly the room gains an additional countertop; then, outfitted with either a cooktop or a second sink, the island offers another prep area and can even double as a breakfast bar. In an L- or U-shaped kitchen, provide aisles that are at least 36 inches wide (42 inches is better) around the island.

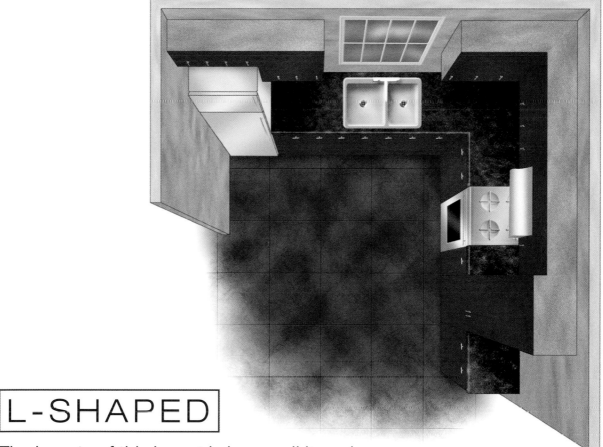

L-SHAPED

The beauty of this layout is how well it works within a limited space; in fact, its two legs use less space than a U-shaped kitchen while still providing a functional and efficient work zone for a single cook. The key is to avoid interrupting the corner of the L: The expanse of countertop should be unbroken. A refrigerator works well at one end when the sink and range are equidistant from its corner. There may even be room in the middle of the kitchen for a small table for casual family meals.

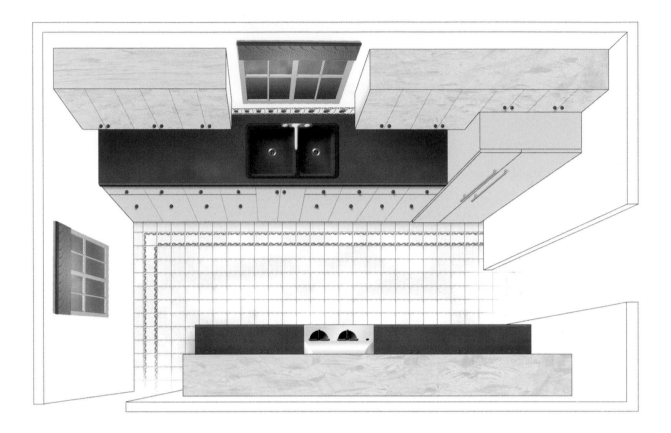

GALLEY

This layout offers maximum efficiency when there's not much space to work with: Its two parallel counters make all points of the work triangle equally accessible. One drawback to a galley is congestion, especially when doors to any appliance or cabinet are open. It's tough for more than two people to cook in this kitchen at the same time. To reduce congestion, make the center aisle 4 to 6 feet wide and place the sink and refrigerator on one wall, with the range on the opposite wall.

WORK CENTER

This relatively new approach creates discrete areas for food preparation, cooking, and cleanup. Like the dual-workstation kitchen (page 19), the arrangement is great for multiple cooks and requires the same enlarged dimensions. Use the island as the prep area, and link the refrigerator and other food storage (including an under counter refrigerator or freezer drawers) to the prep sink and a chopping block. The cooking zone centers around the cooktop and should be outfitted with storage for pots, pans, utensils, cookbooks, and herbs and spices. Wall ovens for baking can occupy a separate corner. To provide a cleanup area, place the main sink, dishwasher, and storage for the dishes, glasses, and flatware nearby.

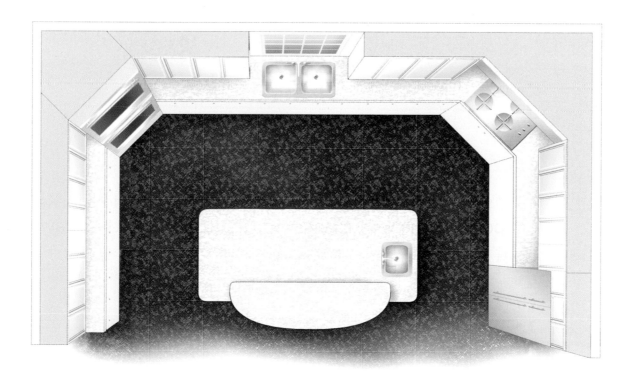

10 TOP KITCHEN PLANNING GUIDELINES

Designing a kitchen is an art—and a science. You'll improve your chances of success if you consider standard planning guidelines. Here are 10 of the most important. For a list of additional guidelines, contact the National Kitchen & Bath Association.

1. For optimum clearance, allow at least 48 inches between cabinets or appliances that face each other.

2. In kitchens smaller than 150 sq. ft., try for at least 13 feet of base cabinets, 12 feet of wall cabinets, and 11 feet of countertops. In kitchens 150 square feet. or larger, go with at least 16 feet of base cabinets, 15½ feet of wall cabinets, and 16½ feet of countertops.

3. Allow 15 to 18 inches between wall and base cabinetry.

4. For maximum convenience, leave at least 24 inches of counter space on one side of the sink and at least 18 inches on the other.

5. To create the most accessible landing for unloading groceries, provide at least 15 inches of counter space on the handle side of a standard refrigerator, or 15 inches on each side if it's a side-by-side model. Or create a landing area on an island or peninsula directly across from the refrigerator, but no more than 48 inches away.

6. For cleanup ease, install the dishwasher within 36 inches of one edge of the sink and provide at least 21 inches of standing room next to it.

7. Provide at least 15 inches of counter near the microwave for prep convenience.

8. To maximize storage, include at least one corner unit of cabinetry.

9. For comfort and to help avoid repetitive-motion injury, plan for work counters of different heights. Counters 28 to 32 inches off the floor are easiest for chopping and seated-use access; those 36 to 45 inches off the floor are best for general tasks (higher counters accommodate taller cooks).

10. When placing a cabinet above the cooktop, provide at least 24 inches of clearance to a fireproof surface, and 30 inches to an unprotected (flammable) surface.

U-SHAPED

With three walls of counter space and storage, this arrangement provides a compact and efficient work area for a single chef. (By locating appliances carefully, two work areas can be created in each corner of the U to accommodate dual cooks.) Though not spacious enough for entertaining, the room can still handle a breakfast table separate from the cooking area. The best plan: Place the refrigerator and cooktop on opposite walls, with the sink centered in the base of the "U."

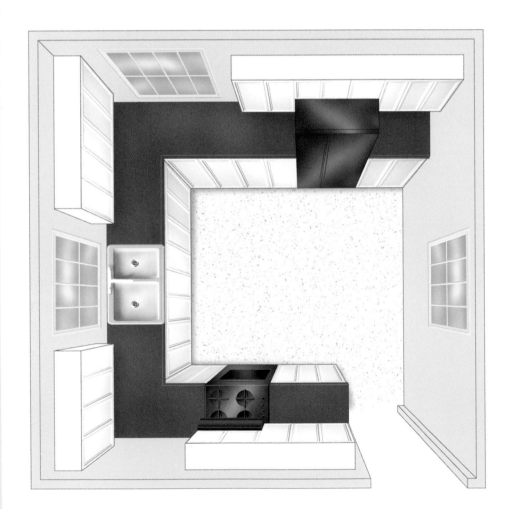

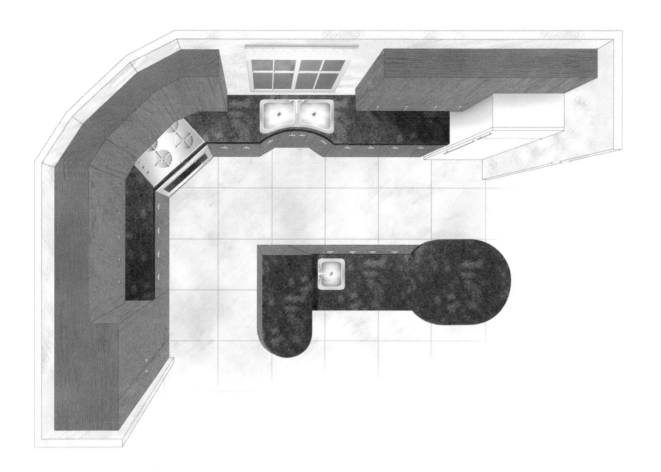

DUAL-WORKSTATION

This is the ideal layout for a two-chef family. But because the goal here is to house two work triangles that don't overlap, this floor plan almost always calls for enlarging the original kitchen or adding a new one. Plan to install a work island or peninsula ample enough to house a prep sink (and possibly a cooktop as well) to partner with the traditional refrigerator/oven/main sink triangle. If there's room, consider putting the microwave oven within the far end of the island to provide a mini-prep/snack area.

Design Ability

Universal design enables any chef to cook in comfort and safety

CONVENTIONAL WISDOM HAS IT THAT STYLE AND practicality go hand in hand, but it took a new design approach to put this concept to work in kitchens. Though it may have emerged from the Americans With Disabilities Act (signed into law in 1990), the universal design movement isn't just for the disabled. Thanks to a forward-thinking design community, it has evolved into an inclusive approach to shaping rooms, particularly kitchens and baths. It places equal value on comfort, efficiency, and aesthetics—for people of all ages and levels of physical capability. In her book *Beautiful Barrier-Free: A Visual Guide to Accessibility* (John Wiley & Sons, 1997), Cynthia Leibrock writes that "accessibility should be the measure of good design rather than the exception to the norm. It should be expected that any well-designed building would provide the minimal amenities of an accessible approach."

The core idea of universal design is this: Any design, whether for a toothbrush, a kitchen counter, or a neighborhood park, will be more comfortable for anyone if it's designed to accommodate the least able person. And considering that by the year 2030 one in five Americans will be over 65, this philosophy couldn't come at a more relevant time.

At its most basic, universal design is about leveling a floor or widening a doorway. But it's also about designing a kitchen drawer to support a fitted top where one can sit in a wheelchair and pay bills or have a snack, for instance. Perhaps because kitchens and baths are the most utilitarian rooms in the house, as well as the site of most household accidents, they stand to gain the most from the application of the universal concept.

"Back in the forties, Mom was the only person expected to be in the kitchen," reads literature from the Universal Kitchen Project at the Rhode Island School of Design. "So the kitchen was standardized for a 5-foot-6-inch-tall woman, probably between 25 and 40 years old. All the components were fixed in place, often out of reach. These days, Mom isn't the only one in the kitchen." The solitary aim of the five-year project, completed in 1998, was to reconsider kitchen standards.

RISD's prototypical kitchen was designed as a "kit" of adjustable and interchangeable parts. The placement and height of refrigeration units, countertop burners, and cabinets could all be adapted to the varying requirements of those using the

The placement of this base cabinet provides easy access to frequently used small appliances, pots, and pans. Its roll-top door doesn't get in the way when open, and when closed, it hides the cabinet's contents from view.

This pullout cabinet table extends to create an accessible area for preparing simple dishes or enjoying a snack. With its false drawer front, it blends in with the cabinetry when closed.

UNIVERSAL GUIDELINES FOR KITCHEN DESIGN

1. Place the most frequently used appliances, equipment, and other elements between 15 and 48 inches off the floor; this is the basic universal reach range.

2. Allow for knee space under sinks and, as a safety precaution, insulate any exposed water pipes beneath the sink.

3. Construct counters in multiple heights around the room. Counters that vary in height from 45 to 28 inches accommodate a tall, standing adult, a child, and a wheelchair user alike.

4. Provide lower cabinets with drawers to eliminate awkward reaching. Outfit upper cabinets with easily adjustable shelving.

5. Equip cabinet doors with touch latches, which make opening them far easier than pulling on knobs or similar hardware.

6. Consider positioning electrical outlets and switches on the sides of cabinetry at a height that can be reached from a seated position; that will make them more accessible than wall placement.

7. Replace double knobs on faucets with single levers, and consider installing sinks that can adjust to different heights.

8. Use adaptable and adjustable ambient lighting, along with task lighting. They should be glare-free.

9. Try to provide turning space for a person using a wheelchair. For a 360- degree turning space, a minimum of 60 by 60 inches is required at floor level.

10. Above all, remember that universally designed spaces do not have to appear clinical and cold in order to be accommodating. They can be gracious, attractive, and stylish.

ABOVE LEFT: This cooktop work center is attractive—and equally accessible to a standing or seated cook. ABOVE: Following the trend for multiple counter heights in kitchens, this arrangement serves a dual purpose: It offers a comfortably high work surface to someone standing, and provides a barrier-free lower level that can be used both for food preparation and informal eating.

space, and all the elements were situated to minimize movement and effort. The designers positioned the oven at countertop height to eliminate the need to bend down. They created a movable cart with a storage area and a surface that can be adjusted to varying heights; this allows someone to prepare, serve, and store food from a seated position. The crisper drawer of the refrigerator was placed near a prep sink, and another sink was designed for both steaming food and washing. The team also designed a "snack center," with a microwave oven and coffee machine, where quick meals could be made easily. All of these features express the basic premise of universal design, says project director Jane Langmuir: "to design for the lifetime, not just the prime time."

Interestingly, pre-19th-century kitchens incorporated more accessibility than many contemporary layouts, and they can provide important cues for designing with a whole lifespan of needs in mind. For

Concealed lights installed above the cabinets reflect off the ceiling and provide a warm decorative effect. Glass front cabinets can be lit to illuminate the interior.

Lighting

A good lighting plan is an important design tool that boosts utility and safety as well as improving comfort and mood. There are three basic categories of lighting: General, or ambient, light is generally provided by one or more overhead fixtures; it produces a level of brightness that is sufficient for many routine activities. Certain chores, however, require extra, more highly focused "task lighting." Pendants over a work surface or halogens tucked under wall cabinets work well. Finally, accent lighting, like that mounted inside a cabinet to illuminate its contents, plays a purely decorative role. Once you determine your lighting requirements, select suitable fixtures.

Hanging pendant lamps can be positioned to provide plenty of light to illuminate tasks. Choose shades that will shield your eyes from glare.

Dimming Systems

Dimmers work by turning the light on and off very rapidly (120 times per second), changing the output by altering the length of time the light is on. When the light is switched off, no energy is consumed, so a dimmed bulb saves energy. And because heat is decreased, bulbs last longer. Dimmers sometimes buzz audibly—that's the bulb filament vibrating. The noisiest buzzing seems to occur at the 50 percent dimmed level.

Dimmable lights offer benefits for almost every kitchen:

- They reduce glare and permit the individual to select the most comfortable light level.
- They offer versatility and ambience control where different activities share space.
- They are cost-effective, producing savings from reduced energy consumption and extended bulb life. Dimming an incandescent bulb to 90 percent of capacity for its entire life will double its longevity.

One way to eliminate shadows cast on work surfaces and light the work directly is to install task lighting (incandescent, fluorescent, or halogen) on the underside of wall cabinets.

starters, old kitchens feature very few built-ins. "This allowed people to arrange the furnishings the way they wanted," says Mary Jo Peterson, a certified kitchen and bath designer, and author of *Universal Kitchen and Bathroom Planning: Design That Adapts to People* (McGraw-Hill, 1998). "That is one of the objectives of universal design." Generally, the kitchen table was in the center of the room, a configuration that offered a secondary, and lower, work space. And open shelving, plate racks, and glass-front cabinetry—all popular, even trendy, kitchen features today—fostered visibility and easy access.

Accessible design shouldn't be limited to the cabinetry, either. When remodeling, take any opportunity to improve entrances to the kitchen. Accessibility challenges posed by an old house include narrow entrances and confining hallways. "In a lot of old houses, you have narrow doorways opening onto narrow hallways," says Charles H. Hoagland, a builder in Lagrangeville, New York, who specializes in historic renovations and reproductions. During one renovation of an early-1900s Colonial farmhouse, he widened all the 2½-foot door frames to 3 feet. What a difference a mere 6 inches can make. "It was easier for everyone to get around," he says. "Once you're renovating an old house, you realize that this kind of design makes sense for anyone, whether you're using a wheelchair or not."

Poor lighting is another characteristic many old houses share, and it can make mobility considerably more challenging for those with impaired vision. "Central overhead lighting was the tradition in centuries-old houses," says Peterson, and it rarely cast sufficient illumination over the entire room. "Sometimes all it takes to correct this, and transform the space, is a more deliberate combination of task and ambient lighting," she adds. Fixtures mounted under the upper cabinets offer one approach to task lighting. They provide even light from the proper angle, enabling someone to see what they're cutting on the countertop. Ambient lighting provides general illumination for the rest of the room. But the two types of lighting must be balanced so that neither one overwhelms the other. If the ambient lighting is too intense, for example, it will throw shadows just where you don't want them: on the countertops.

For older people and others who have a hard time distinguishing colors, adding more, or brighter, task lighting, specifically in darker areas of the kitchen, may be what's needed. "We tend to adapt to our environment," Peterson adds, "when what we really need to do is make our environment adapt to us."

Appliances

The basic lineup of kitchen equipment—cooktop, refrigerator, oven, and dishwasher—hasn't changed much over the years, but the way we use appliances certainly has. Options in style and size, coupled with new technologies, have made it possible to meet the needs, preferences, or space limitations of any serious cook. Appliances at all price points include enhancements once reserved for the very top end of the market. The model you buy today, no matter how inexpensive, is likely to offer more features and be more efficient, quieter, and better organized than a comparable unit from just a few years ago.

LEFT: With plenty of capacity, side-by-side refrigerator/freezers allow anyone access to at least part of each compartment.
ABOVE: Dishwasher drawers are designed to fit a standard diswasher opening. They can be installed in pairs or individually, and eliminate the need to maneuver around a standard drop-down door.
BELOW LEFT: Wall ovens provide cooking flexibility by combining bake, roast, and broil modes with convection and microwave capabilities.

Living Amenities

Upscale features from bygone eras can improve kitchen efficiency

FAMILY LIFE IS BACK IN STYLE, AND SO ARE FAMILY HOMES. Though they can take as many shapes as there are types and sizes of families, one common feature is this: a flexible interior that reflects a family's interests and activities. When those turn toward cooking or entertaining, the kitchen takes prominence. Lately, some families have rediscovered amenities once found only in the houses of the wealthy.

THE BUTLER'S PANTRY

In the waning days of summer 1941, Florence Crane, widow of one of Chicago's richest industrial tycoons, held a luncheon at her 54-room vacation house. Seated around a table garnished with garden flowers and embroidered doilies, her guests finished the last of their brandied peaches as the hostess silently signaled for the final course. From his post in the pantry, the butler issued one command and a stream of servants filed into the dining room bearing pewter bowls of peppermint ice cream, followed by platters of coconut balls, nectarines, and grapes. Another of Crane's seamless mealtime performances neared its conclusion.

By comparison, today's social gatherings are modest, informal affairs. Barbecues, sushi parties, and martini mixers have replaced eight-course dinners. If necessary, we hire caterers and valets for the night; we don't keep them on staff. But while the perfectly poised, ever-ready butler has become a thing of the past, his pantry is making a comeback.

"Every house we've done in recent memory has a butler's pantry," says McKee Patterson, an architect in Southport, Connecticut. None match the gymnasium-size pantry of the Crane estate, yet the modern butler's pantry serves essentially the same function as its predecessor: It provides space for storing the finer service—china, glassware, and silver (the kitchen pantry holds foodstuffs)—and acts as a buffer zone between the dining room and kitchen. "It's a staging area," says Patterson, "a place to prepare platters and plates and drinks, and to drop them off when you're done." That's why the butler's pantry has always had plenty of counter and cabinet space and at least one sink, but may these days include even a refrigerator and dishwasher.

Before World War II, those who could afford opulent mansions and scores of servants had spacious butler's pantries to receive food from the kitchen and dirty dishware from the dining room. Like any good butler's pantry, the one at the Crane estate has an abundance of counter space and storage. The Cranes' best place settings were stored on the pantry's upper level.

ABOVE: *This Old House* host Steve Thomas borrowed the butler's pantry at the Watertown project house to cook up some hard-shelled New England delicacies. Seperated from the kitchen by a chest-high granite countertop and beadboard wainscoting, the pantry serves as an all-purpose prep station and cleanup area. To Steve's right, a pull out waste-basket hides behind oak paneling.

To some extent, the resurgence of the butler's pantry is about nostalgia, a fascination with the seemingly gracious domestic life of the late-19th and early-20th centuries. "The butler's pantry, like bedroom 'chambers' and maid's rooms, is the perfect example of the 'paraphernalia of gentility,'" says Standish Meacham, professor emeritus of history at the University of Texas at Austin. Sandra Fairbank, architect for the 1998 *This Old House* project in Watertown, Massachusetts, thinks the butlerless butler's pantry may also be a response to the hectic pace of everyday living. "Life is fast and people work so hard," she says.

Fairbank designed a butler's pantry for the owners of the Watertown house, Christian Nolen and Susan Denny, as a way to connect the high-tech 1990s kitchen to the rest of the 1886 Victorian. Strategically placed between the dining room and the kitchen, the pantry mixes modern and traditional elements: quartersawn oak cabinets next to a stainless-steel dishwasher; glass-front cupboards facing an integral stainless steel sink and drain board; and a beadboard backsplash above thick granite countertops. It's not a huge space—just 9 feet by 9 feet—but the compactness means there's little wasted motion.

So far, Denny insists that she can manage without a butler. "The pantry itself is such a help," she says. "We had a dinner party recently, and we were able to bus things in and out very efficiently. The whole night flowed really well." Just the way Florence Crane would have liked it.

THE DUMBWAITER

With two teenage boys in the house, Laura Roney spends a lot of time washing a dirty clothes. So when she and her husband, Patrick, began planning their new home, she asked the architect to locate the laundry room upstairs near the bedrooms, so she wouldn't have to cart the heavy loads up and down the stairs. After sketching a solution, though, he told her that the washer and dryer wouldn't fit anywhere but the basement. "He suggested a laundry chute," says Laura. "I looked at him and said, 'But that goes only one way!'"

Instead, they installed a dumbwaiter. And in the months after the Roneys moved into their new home, this mini-elevator took the heavy lifting out of Laura's laundry day. It carries soiled clothes and linens down to the basement from the second floor, and after they're washed and folded, delivers them back upstairs.

This may sound a little like modern technology solving an age-old problem, but it isn't. Thomas Jefferson installed two dumbwaiters at Monticello. And by the Victorian era, these vertical valets had become must-have features for upscale row houses, ferrying food prepared in the first-floor kitchens to the dining rooms above. They fell out of favor only in the mid-20th century, as house styles flattened out, but with so many multistory homes now being built on small lots, and so many boomers nursing aging knees and backs, dumbwaiters are back in style for both renovations and new homes. Along with being laundry luggers, dumbwaiters can carry groceries from the garage to the kitchen or firewood from the basement to the living room.

RIGHT: In their kitchen, Nancy and Larry Rice use an electric dumbwaiter, hidden behind a door that matches the cabinetry, to haul their groceries from the garage below.
INSET: The dumbwaiter also helps with laundry duties. Downstairs, its door opens next to the washer and dryer.

The modern dumbwaiter is little more than a boxlike metal cab that rides up and down a vertical shaftway on two aluminum rails. A cable-and-pulley system connects the cab to a hand-operated rope or an electric motor. Manual models, which typically cost $3,000 to $6,500 (installed), use counterweights, so it takes little effort to lift loads up to 250 pounds. Electric dumbwaiters have a reversible ½- to 2-horsepower motor that sits at the top or bottom of the shaft, winding and unwinding steel cable. At $6,000 to $20,000 (installed), they offer greater capacity—up to 500 pounds—and faster service.

To operate a manual dumbwaiter, you open the outer doors and pull on the rope. A brake holds the cab in position when you're not pulling. Motorized models have safety brakes, too. Some systems even "sense" a jammed cab, shutting the motor down when the cable goes slack or when an excessive load is placed on the motor.

The shaftway—typically a 2-by-2-foot chase framed with 2x4s and lined with one-hour-fire-rated drywall—is simple to incorporate into the plans for a new house or addition. But adding one to an existing home can get tricky. Space can sometimes be found in the chases once used for furnace air returns, or in abandoned chimneys, or even in long-gone dumbwaiters. Another possibility is to build a shaft on the outside of the house or run it through closets positioned one over the other. A fire can spread quickly up a chase, so Robinson recommends installing a smoke detector at its top.

The dumbwaiter itself is typically sold in a kit containing everything the contractor needs to install the system—hardware, motor, rails, doors, cab, pulleys, and cables. After installation, it should be given a routine maintenance check by the installer about every two to three years for hand-operated models, annually for electric. "If homeowners notice that any of the safety devices are not working," says Bill McMichael, general manager for Waupaca Elevator Company, "they should have them fixed right away."

Safety wasn't a major concern for Ginger and Jack Knutsen when they added a dumbwaiter to their Seattle home. ("I use it for laundry, to haul flower-arranging supplies up and down, and to just carry stuff around," says Ginger.) But that was before their two rambunctious grandsons tried to take it for a ride. Luckily, they were caught climbing in. (These systems aren't kidproof, but installing locking doors more than 36 inches off the floor should keep children out.) "If I were their age," says Ginger with a chuckle. "I'd probably have tried that myself."

Islands in The Kitchen

Creative ideas and tips for storage and cooking efficiency

ABOUT 30 YEARS AGO, THE PENINSULA COUNTER BROKE off from the wall to become an island. Since then, this piece of cabinetry has gone from being an additional work surface to becoming the kitchen's center of gravity. Gradually, various kitchen tasks, pieces of equipment, and social activities have migrated to it, and now it's a culinary center, storage unit, family gathering spot, and entertainment area all in one.

Kitchen islands are immensely popular, but that doesn't mean an island is right for everyone or for every situation. Placed thoughtlessly, it can turn a logical floor plan into a maze. It's also possible to be overwhelmed by an island's sheer potential, warns designer/contractor Richard Baronio: "If there's too much going on, no one part has enough space to function properly."

When planning an island, there are a several practical considerations to keep in mind:

• The kitchen must be large enough to allow at least 36 inches of clearance for traffic lanes on all sides of the island.

• If you want the island to function simultaneously as a place for working and socializing, that's no problem as long as these activities are segregated. The design should discourage milling guests from distracting a busy cook. That's more than a convenience—it's essential for the sake of everyone's safety.

• Arrange the island's features logically—if the dishwasher is in the island, for instance, a sink should be there, too.

• Pay attention to mechanical requirements. Providing a vent for the sink can be tricky; exhaust ventilation for a range or cooktop requires planning and a bigger budget.

• The island itself can be built as a single piece of cabinetry, but it's often far less expensive to assemble it from a collection of stock cabinets attached to each other.

Here are six kitchen islands that illustrate uncommon solutions to kitchen planning problems.

SERIOUS FOOD

The gourmand owners of this kitchen (lower right) needed an island big enough to accommodate multiple tasks. The countertop is granite—a cool surface for rolling pastry—and there's a pull-up shelf for a large dough mixer near the stove top, as well as conventional drawer and cabinet storage for utensils and spices. Pots and pans hang within easy reach from an overhead rack, and there's a prep sink at the far end of the island. One ingenious feature: Undercounter storage for a sideboard cart,

RIGHT: This island, clad with beadboard paneling and topped with a zinc countertop, was designed for a good aesthetic fit with the 1890s brownstone it was built for.

ABOVE: **The open design of this island disguises its considerable mass, yet still offers a buffer to shield kitchen clutter from the dining area. Pendant lighting provides illumination for the cooking surfaces. Fireslate countertop surfaces match the color of slate flooring found elsewhere in the house.**

LEFT: This hard-working island is big enough to accommodate separate areas for simultaneous baking, cooking, and food preparation.

so culinary creations can be wheeled straight into the dining room.

PERIOD PIECE

The owners of an 1890s brownstone in Brooklyn, New York, wanted an island (above left) that would suit the house stylistically. It also had to be multitalented, functioning as a counter for food preparation and disposal, a bar for casually elegant adult dining, and a center to accommodate the everyday culinary needs of children.

They chose oak beadboard as the skin of the island, and stained it to match woodwork found elsewhere in the house. There's also a zinc countertop, a material chosen for its strong vintage associations (stainless steel would have seemed much too high-tech). Despite the antique ambiance of the island, however, it contains one thoroughly 20th-century piece of equipment—a dishwasher is hidden on the island's far side.

SPLIT LEVEL

This island (above) was designed to separate the kitchen from a dining area, and had to house large appliances—including an inset stove and an under-counter oven. But it also had to provide counter seating. To achieve all this, Michaela Mahady, of

SALA Architects designed a bar that floats on fins above the main island countertop, which breaks up the island's bulk and partially screens off messes on the lower working surface. Both countertops are made of Fireslate, a cementitious material that feels cool to the touch. The island includes storage drawers and a slide-out surface intended for a laptop computer.

HEAVENLY ISLAND

It was pity, not love, that drew Matthew Cox to buy the derelict but historic house on one of Houston's oldest streets. "I'm kind of a sucker when it comes to the stray dog or cat," he says, "and this house definitely needed help." Indeed, it had no heat, no plumbing, and no electricity.

Eventually, Cox restored the house to the point where it was not only livable, but lovable. It even earned a place on the National Register of Historic Places. The house originated as lodging for railroad workers in the 1860s, and the kitchen thus remains suitably modest (facing page). Except, of course, for the kitchen island. Parked beneath a restored Victorian light fixture, the 1850s pulpit sports a new marble top. Along with it's strictly utilitarian duties, the pulpit/island serves as a reminder that most any house can be saved.

ISLAND VIEW

In designing this island (top left) for a Lake Superior lodge, architect Dale Mulfinger provided a transition between the kitchen and the great room beyond. The use of light woods helps to create a seamless visual whole. Sitting neatly between two columns, the island provides a buffet area and extra bar-type seating at the overhanging counter. Rather than position the stove against the back wall, Mulfinger slotted it into the kitchen side of the island. That way, anyone at the stove gets to enjoy a wonderful view towards the lake.

PLAIN AND SIMPLE

This appliance-free island (left), designed by Jerome Buttrick of Buttrick Architects, provides a clean, uncluttered work surface with undercounter storage between a kitchen and a dining room. "White wood and mahogany trim is the motif of the house, so the countertop is a 1½-inch slab of mahogany with a tung oil–based sealer," says the owner of the house. Cabinet doors on the dining-room side conceal drawers for table linens, and the ends of the island incorporate open shelves for cookbooks. The raised area of the countertop serves as a sideboard, and it also hides any work-surface mess from dining-table view.

FACING PAGE: The visual highlight of this simple kitchen is an island made from an antique pulpit.
ABOVE: The island for this lakeside lodge nestles between two 6x6 support posts.
LEFT: This straightforward island incorporates clean design details. Note how the backsplash of the countertop behind takes its visual cues from the island's panel doors.

Looking for Some Help?

Meet the professionals who can design and build your new kitchen

For relatively small spaces, kitchens require a whole lot of specialists when remodeling time comes around. The process begins with the designer—the person with the ideas—and ends with the contractor—the person who builds the project. Here's who you can call on to help with your project.

ARCHITECTS

You hire an architect to listen to your wish list, solve design problems, and prepare construction drawings. Depending on your project, you may choose to hire one to oversee the entire project, too. Although their work is spatially and aesthetically driven, the real art of their job may be in anticipating each step of the project and planning it creatively. To become licensed, architects must spend at least three years as an intern, then pass a state exam that tests for knowledge of local and national construction standards. Licensed architects are required to complete a certain number of hours of continuing education, the frequency of which varies per state. Membership in the American Institute of Architects (AIA) is optional, though the organization keeps members up-to-date on design policies and provides current contracts.

TIP: Select someone who designs kitchen regularly, has designed spaces that you would like to live in, and whose work is known by the local review board.

BUILDING DESIGNERS

Like architects, they are able to understand how the kitchen relates, structurally and aesthetically, to the entire house. Often designers have been trained as architects but have not been licensed as architects by the state. Some may also have backgrounds in interior design or construction.

TIP: Those accredited by the American Institute of Building Designers—which issues the Professional Building Designer designation—have passed a competency exam; they must also complete eight hours of continuing education each year. Unaccredited building designers may be just as experienced; the background of any professional should be verified.

CERTIFIED KITCHEN DESIGNERS

They specialize in this work and must adhere to design and safety guidelines issued by the National Kitchen and Bath Association (NKBA). To become certified by the NKBA, a designer must

QUESTIONS FOR ANYONE YOU HIRE

Begin the selection process by interviewing at least three professionals in both the design and building fields. (If you are planning to be your own general contractor, this extends to each of the subcontractors as well.) Take the time to visit their completed projects and talk with past clients. Check with the Better Business Bureau or the local chapter of the appropriate trade organizations to see if any litigation is pending against them, and always ask the following questions:

- How long have you been in business?
- Do you have insurance? May I see a copy of the certificates?
- May I see a copy of your license or certification?
- Do you provide a contract?
- How do you guarantee your work?
- Will you give me a detailed written bid?
- Will you arrange for the building permit?
- May I talk to the building-material suppliers with whom you frequently work?
- Who are the subcontractors with whom you regularly work? May I call them?
- Is there a pager, cell phone, or other means of contacting you in a timely way?
- Do you provide a certificate of completion?

"Decide what you need and can afford, then check out your contractor. How long has he been in business? Is he insured? Is he a local— someone who will have to live with his work? Investigate, think, then make up your own mind. It's the only way."

— NORM ABRAM

pass an exam and complete 15 hours of continuing education every three years.

TIP: You may want to hire a contractor to work with your CKD because the designer might lack a broader understanding of structural concerns and building codes as they pertain to adjacent rooms.

INTERIOR DESIGNERS

Interior designers are acquainted with the latest trends, products, and decorating materials, and they have a strong aesthetic sense of how various elements work together. Like other design professionals, they often have an alliance with a contractor who executes their work.

TIP: Accreditation from the American Society of Interior Designers (ASID) means that the individual holds a two- or four-year degree in design, has at least two years of field experience, and has passed a six-part exam. But there are many well-respected designers who are not ASID-accredited, so this shouldn't be your only criterion.

BUILDING PROFESSIONALS

These folks pick up where the design pro leaves off. They understand your home's structure, pay attention to safety issues, comply with building codes, and get the necessary permits.

Contractors: There are general contractors and specialty contractors. General contractors are adept at hiring, scheduling, coordinating, and overseeing all the specialty contractors (called subcontractors) who actually do the work. Homeowners who elect to serve as their own general contractors can hire the various subs directly, but must be prepared to spend the time working out schedules and solving problems with each one.

TIP: Some contractors belong to either the National Association of Home Builders (NAHB) Remodelers Council or the National Association of the Remodeling Industry (NARI). Membership requires a certain number of years of field experience. More important is choosing a someone who is licensed by state or local government and has insurance that covers both himself and those he hires.

Design/build firms: These are building companies that have an in-house architect or designer as well as construction crews—an arrangement that streamlines the design and construction process and resolves conflicts between both parties more easily, because they are on the same team.

TIP: Because the designer is working closely with the contractor, construction details are typically worked out in advance. On the other hand, creativity can be compromised in favor of construction speed and practicality.

You Got a Permit for That?

Call it helpful attention from the government or Big Brother watching, but when you build, renovate, or add on, town hall wants to know what you're up to

MENTION BUILDING PERMITS, AND you're likely to hear tales of red tape, stalled renovations, and thwarted dreams. During the six-month ordeal of one homeowner, various boards and bureaucrats layered demands onto the project, including, at one point, a request for a firetruck turnaround so large it would have required demolishing the house. And one New York City landlord remembers when applying for a building permit meant showing up with a cash-filled envelope to motivate crooked bureaucrats to green-light a construction project. "We used to call it 'giving to the church,'" he recalls.

Yet despite their bad reputation, building permits make sense. "People don't realize that it's to their own benefit to get a building permit," says *This Old House* contractor Tom Silva. Permits protect the public's interests and ensure the safety of homeowners. Requirements vary among states and municipalities, but town officials generally want to review any renovation plan that enlarges a living space or involves the house's mechanicals—plumbing, heating, electricity—to make sure it meets local building codes. Drawings showing your intended alterations may also be kicked to other departments, such as those in charge of zoning and environmental protection, which might set limits on the project. Once a permit is issued and posted on the job site, inspectors will keep an eye on the work as it progresses.

And scary stories aside, the process usually works smoothly. Payoffs are no longer routine, and it may even be possible to obtain a permit within days. While it never hurts to hire an architect or contractor who is well thought of by your building department, it's not essential. In Oxford, Connecticut, for example, town hall maintains evening hours, and one night architect Roger van Loveren, of Bedford, New York, and his client walked in to find the building, health, wetlands, and zoning officials all in their offices. Architect and client left ecstatic, with necessary permits in hand.

Still, about 30 percent of renovating homeowners don't apply for permits, according to Bob Kelly, of the National Conference of States on Building Codes and Standards. They may fear delays and government interference, but the most common reason is that they don't want the tax assessor to get wind of the improvements. That typically results in a property tax increase, especially if the project adds a bedroom or some other highly marketable feature. If you're planning a remodel, you'll have to decide whether to get a

permit or renovate on the sly. Being a renovation renegade can be tempting because of the time and money you may save in the short run, but going without a permit may ultimately make your life more complicated.

Trying to skirt a permit is a dangerous game. Only about 20 to 30 percent of homeowners get away with it, says Kelly: "It depends on where you live. If you're in Tall Timber, West Virginia, down a private logging road, chances of anyone noticing your project are pretty slim. But if you're in the middle of suburbia and you're six feet away from your neighbors, they might be curious and call the local building department and say, 'Hey, do you know about the work going on next door?'" Projects involving a knockdown, creation of a more imposing structure, or construction near a waterway are most likely to raise suspicions. Also, town officials like to keep their eyes out for Dumpsters and collections of pickup trucks—telltale signs of a construction project. Get caught, and you'll have to call an expensive halt to the project while you apply for the permit.

Worse still, you may have to undo the work—a lesson one of Tom Silva's customers learned the hard way some 25 years ago. "He insisted on a deck that didn't fit. It was supposed to be fifteen feet back from the property line," Silva recalls. "I tried to talk him out of it, but he wanted to take his chances so I reluctantly built it, then had to take it down and redo it at his expense. I will never work without a permit again."

Even if you complete the project without getting caught, an uninspected renovation can block the sale of the house years later. In some municipalities, before you can sell, you need the building department to issue a certificate of occupancy to prove that the house is free of code violations. If officials discover that the home is different from the description on record and that no permits were issued for the alterations, they won't grant the "CO" until you satisfy the building inspector, who may knock holes in the walls to conduct an inspection or even order you to remove the improvement. (If you do risk going without a permit, make sure the work is done to code anyway and photograph the essentials before the walls are closed up—you'll need it as proof later.)

For Michelle Mabry, there was no question of whether or not to get a permit when she renovated her kitchen. But she didn't realize that her permit would trigger 11 inspections and that the city wanted her to be home for each one. But it's the owner's interests that are being served by making sure the contractor's work is up to par, and because the owner's presence helps deter the inspector from getting cozy with the builder and approving poor construction. Now Mabry can sit in her gorgeous kitchen and know that it was built completely to code. Her home is safe, she needn't ever worry that her neighbors will tattle about surreptitious work, and she has the papers to prove the value added to the house—in her opinion, those were all worth the effort. ∎

KEEPING NEIGHBORHOODS NICE

Some communities require renovation projects to meet aesthetic standards as well as safety and zoning codes. About 2,300 historic district commissions across the country, as well as hundreds of architectural review boards and neighborhood associations, limit changes to the exteriors of houses within their boundaries. Most have the power to stop work and levy fines. In Alexandria, Virginia, for instance, starting demolition without a permit from the historic district commission can lead to fines of $1,500 per day per offense, says city architect Al Cox. By protecting properties from ugly renovations, these boards help to preserve neighborhood character and property values. Problem is, legislating things like roofing materials and paint colors is a subjective job; board members' individual tastes and the aggressiveness of neighbors can sway decisions.

When Deborah and Kevin Guinee renovated their 18th-century Salem, Massachusetts, home in 1995 with *This Old House*, their permit required review by a historic district commission. Their plans called for sacrificing a rear side room in

order to cut a carriage-style archway through the house so that they could park in the backyard. But a cluster of neighborhood naysayers was so vocal at public hearings that the Guinees withdrew their proposal.

"As much as you wouldn't want politics to influence planning decisions, it always does," says Pratt Cassity, executive director of the National Alliance of Preservation Commissions. "And it's especially true in older communities where the houses are close together."

Architect Jerry Zimmer, who designed the *This Old House* renovation in Santa Barbara, California, says, "If you're sensitive to what the boards want, it's not hard at all." Use a local architect and engineer who know the board members and are likely to design passable plans. "Someone from out of town who wants to do something avant garde or daring may run afoul of the board," says Zimmer. Cassity's advice: To help make sure you win approval from the board, win over the neighbors first. "Deal with it the old-fashioned way—invite them over for a drink," he says.

Before

&After

NEW WAYS TO THINK ABOUT YOUR OLD KITCHEN

WHAT ANYONE, ON ANY BUDGET, HOPES FOR IN A KITCHEN remodel is this: Transformation. It is the same for resourceful do-it-yourselfers and hands-off hire-it-outers. But every effort pays off when dreary, awkward spaces turn bright and efficient, and the budget hasn't been busted, and dinner is underway again at last. How does this happen? Ask Steve Thomas, the host of *This Old House*. Several years ago he began a collaboration with editors of *This Old House* magazine to showcase successful kitchen projects. The goal: to demonstrate how to get from "Before" to happily ever "After." Here you'll find the best of these projects, including a pro-grade kitchen packed into a bare 100 s.f. and one with cabinets that cost less than $100. Read on and you'll find another hope of kitchen remodelers: inspiration.

Blond Ambition

Without adding on, light and space were found for a cramped kitchen

THE SAGA BEGAN WHEN THE TRUSTY OLD 40-INCH-WIDE stove went on the fritz and couldn't be repaired. Up until then, the owners of the postwar ranch house just outside of Boston had not paid much attention to the kitchen. In fact, while they were raising their two children, it had suited them just fine. The kitchen's dark pine cabinets, plastic laminate countertops, almond appliances, and orange wallpaper were way past their prime, but the L-shape layout was reasonably efficient, and the style of the room meshed with the design of the rest of the house.

The demise of the stove—and the departure of their now-grown children—forced the couple to take stock of the kitchen. It was time for a change—but how much of one? After several weeks of discussions, the couple decided to reorganize the work triangle, while updating the look of the room by using contemporary versions of the old materials. A call to Peter Lawton, of DesignPlus Kitchens & Baths, in Worcester, Massachusetts, set the project in motion.

PROBLEM

"A 16-by-12-foot kitchen isn't enormous to begin with," says *This Old House* host Steve Thomas. Exploding the footprint would have been the easy way out, but it wasn't an option in this case. The property couldn't accommodate an addition, and the couple didn't want to pay for a huge remodel. "They gave me strict instructions," Lawton recalls: "Retain the basic shape of the room, and preserve the doorways."

SOLUTION

Lawson had to look for space where he could get it. Working off the room's original footprint, the designer suggested two practical alterations to the L-shape layout: First, remove the wall the kitchen shared with the cellar stairs (and against which an old breakfast table and chairs used to stand) and create a "working wall" that incorporates two cabinets, a counter for the couple's cookbooks, and a microwave oven. Second, "kick out" a 6-foot peninsula at a 45-degree angle from the main counter area, which runs between the window and the back door. The

The new kitchen is fairly compact—even after adding a peninsula (and an extra bank of cabinets), everything fits perfectly.

BEFORE

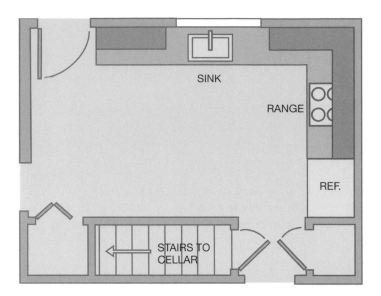

AFTER

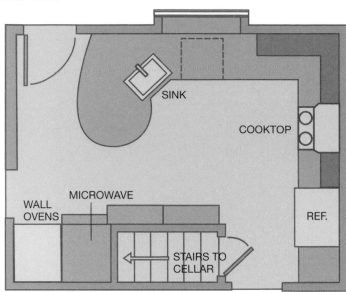

peninsula would provide a cozy spot for eating, as well as a convenient drop-off spot for groceries. The sink, previously under the window, migrated to the peninsula to create a continuous work surface between it and a new cooktop.

Adding these features to the kitchen, of course, lopped off some floor space. In order to compensate, Lawton "used some great design tricks to make the room feel more spacious," says Steve. For one, the designer removed an antiquated steel casement window and replaced it with a custom-made greenhouse window that bumps out 10 inches. He then extended the granite countertop to fill the window recess. "By creating a kind of niche, he gave the illusion of depth to a narrow space," says Steve.

To add "height" to the room, Lawton ran a soffit along three sides of the ceiling. The eye is also drawn upward by the unbroken swath of granite that extends from the countertop to link the upper and lower cabinets.

FINISHING TOUCHES

Lawton realized that the materials and decorative elements in the kitchen would have to work just as hard as any organizational sleight of hand to transform the room into a cheerful, modern space. To "go retro, but with a contemporary twist," Lawton chose materials that were a throwback to the postwar era of the house's construction. "Those were the years of the blond-birch cabinet, but we used maple here," he says. "To mimic the flagstone

The granite countertop and backsplash are extremely durable, and contrast nicely with the cabinets.

Double ovens occupy a former closet. Two cabinets next to it are punctuated by a granite counter that functions as a "trivet" for the microwave.

that was used a lot in those days, we went with slate flooring. And the opaque glass on the cabinet fronts reminds me of public buildings from the time."

Lawton also chose stainless-steel appliances with a look that seemed slightly old-fashioned, rather than commercial. A professional-style built-in cooktop, like those used in old diners, dropped into the same space occupied by the old "oven-and-a-half," while the couple's capacious stainless-steel refrigerator stayed put. Retaining the positions of these appliances was a smart budget move; gas and electric lines servicing them didn't need to be moved.

The lighting, on the other hand, is purely modern—halogen lights recessed into the soffit. Lawton chose low-voltage incandescent light to work a different trick under the cabinets—to warm up the appearance of the dark granite.

Manipulating all the design elements in such an efficient manner puts everything in the kitchen within easy reach. It works to the owners' advantage in human terms, too: One of the things they love most about the room is having a quiet dinner together at the peninsula.

UP FOR GRABS

One of the distinctive features of this kitchen is the use of extra-long stainless-steel pulls on the cabinets and drawers (facing page). The pulls are "another space-enhancing touch," says *T.O.H.* host Steve Thomas, who admires the way they emphasize the shape of each unit. These were semi-customized by the manufacturer for this job. Other long and distinctive pulls are widely available, though.

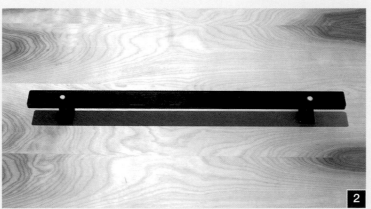

CLOCKWISE FROM ABOVE:
1. This forged-steel, three-piece "straight reed" pull measures 18 inches overall. 2. A sleek and flat 20-inch pull. 3. This slender "bow" pull ranges in length from a compact 1¼ inches to 8 inches. 4. Matte-black "steel railing" pulls range up to 54 inches long.

Light Touch

A gloomy kitchen gets turned into a sunny gathering spot for the family

S TANDING IN ANN AND PETER HOWLEY'S NEWLY renovated kitchen, Steve Thomas taps his fingers on a gleaming counter. "Nice stuff," he says. "I love the way the brass drawer pulls pick up flecks of mica in the green-black granite." Steve shakes his head as he gazes at photos of the depressing kitchen that once occupied this space. "I can see how previous owners tried to turn a warren of little rooms into a family room-kitchen area, but they never solved the problem of poor light and awkward traffic flow," he notes. "Now the kitchen and sitting room are the best parts of the house."

Five years earlier, when the Howleys moved into their 1926 Tudor in Wellesley, Massachusetts, they were charmed by the six-bedroom house, which sits on a hill and is surrounded by old-growth oak trees and rolling lawns providing plenty of room for their Standard poodles Harvey and Grady to dart around. But the kitchen needed help. "It wasn't so much the kitchen's functionality—it worked okay," Ann says. "But, Lord, it was dark and ugly."

RIGHT: Highlights of this kitchen renovation include an island with a recessed pastry counter. BELOW: The old mock-Tudor kitchen and the family room lacked adequate light, appealing fixtures, and a workable layout.

PROBLEM

Steve nods in agreement, pointing out that "small windows and dark wood floors made this room utterly gloomy." Despite a redo in the '70s—complete with laminate countertops, walnut-stained cabinets, and fake foam ceiling beams—the

kitchen was not a place where anyone would want to spend a lot of time. "There was so much potential to enlarge it and open it up," says Steve, "when you consider that they had a seldom-used study, a screened-in porch, and a laundry area sitting on the other side of the stairs." Those stairs, though, sat behind a wall that divided the space in half and prevented the sunlight on one side of the house from reaching the other side.

SOLUTION

Says Steve, "As soon as the Howleys bought the house, they knew they were going to have to do something about the

hulking staircase in the middle of the room." He wondered why the stairs hadn't been removed entirely since there were two ways to go up. But then, he says, "the Howleys told me how much they used this route, and I could see that the architect's solution to remove the enclosure and reverse the direction of the stairs was a better idea—and not too expensive because they could retain the structural opening and just rebuild the steps."

Treff LaFleche, an architect with LDA Architects in Cambridge, Massachusetts, devised the plan. "Instead of being hidden behind a wall, the stairs now cascade into the middle of the room," says LaFleche. Ann thought about displaying her collection of 18th-century curio plates and molds

By building the steps to rise in the other direction and taking down the wall that enclosed them, a clunky staircase was turned into the architectural centerpiece of the enlarged kitchen and sitting room, creating open sight lines between the two rooms.

on the oak ledges, which extend horizontally along the exposed kitchen side of the staircase. But she decided this architectural detail stood on its own as abstract art.

In the cramped kitchen, LaFleche stripped out the dark paneling, cabinetry, and flooring, ripped out the L-shaped counter, and replaced the space-eating cast-iron radiators with thin-tubed, forced-hot-water heat in the cabinet toekicks and along the baseboard. On the other side of the stairs, he demolished walls to claim the porch and study for a sitting room, and the laundry area for a butler's pantry. (The washer and dryer were relegated to the basement.) LaFleche had fluted columns built to frame the entrances between the kitchen and adjacent

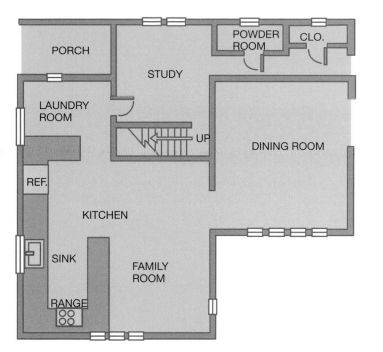

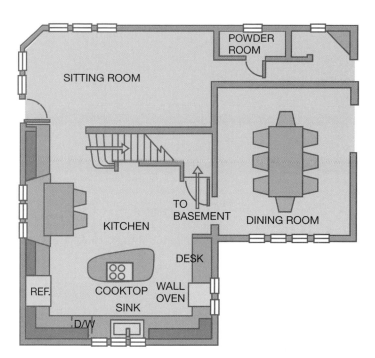

rooms, which Steve says "retain the division of space without isolating one area from another." To bring in more natural light, the architect replaced small diamond-paned and casement windows with larger double-hung ones spaced proportionately all around.

By absorbing the old family room, he expanded the kitchen, edging it with 33 feet of counters that culminate in a built-in desk near the dining room. An asymmetrical, curved island—supported by a wooden leg to make it seem like furniture—features a four-burner gas cooktop. One corner of the island drops to a height of 30 inches (as opposed to 36 inches) to accommodate Ann's frequent baking.

FINISHING TOUCHES

Wanting a "crisp, clean" country look, the couple settled on an oak floor with a brownish-black stain, black granite counters, and white painted cabinets, some with glass fronts. LaFleche added recessed halogens and spotlights. "Smart task lighting is a must for any serious cook," says Steve. "I also like the mini-butler's pantry between the kitchen and sitting room—it's convenient without yelling 'I'm new! I'm modern.' The Howleys now have a kitchen that functions well yet looks like it belongs in a 1920s house."

Brass drawer pulls accentuate the mica highlights scattered throughout the granite countertops.

Beauty On a Budget

Secondhand cabinets are the key to this sleek, chic kitchen redo

W HEN KELTON AND SARAH OSBORN MARRIED and bought a starter house in the Park Hill section of Denver, Colorado, in 1998, they were attracted by its low price and its location—five minutes from both their offices—not by its design. Says Kelton bluntly of the 1925 brick bungalow: "There was really nothing unique or special about the place."

That was particularly true of the kitchen. The Osborns were eager to create an attractive cooking and dining space, but they had a modest budget—around $7,000. With the average kitchen renovation costing $25,000 to $30,000, according to the National Kitchen and Bath Association, and half of that typically going to cabinetry alone, they knew they were going to have to be creative.

PROBLEM

The 1,000-square-foot bungalow was broken up into boxlike rooms, but the couple preferred more open spaces. At 9 by 12 feet, the kitchen had sufficient size, but it was poorly organized

ABOVE: An inefficient layout and a dated look were among the reasons to renovate this boxy kitchen. RIGHT: Now open to the dining area, the space is airier and far more functional, making entertaining easy.

and outdated. "It didn't make sense to keep the old kitchen," says Kelton. "There wasn't much counter space or storage, there was no dishwasher, and the cabinets had who knows how many layers of paint on them. We decided to tear it all out and start over."

Besides creating an efficient work space, the couple wanted

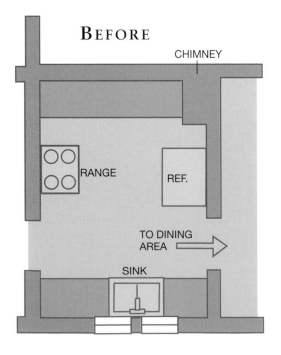

BEFORE

CHIMNEY

RANGE

REF.

TO DINING AREA →

SINK

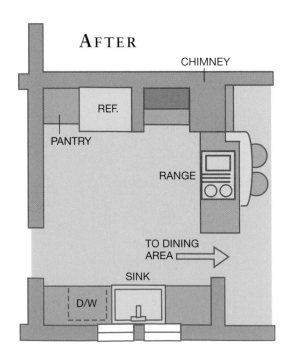

AFTER

CHIMNEY

REF.

PANTRY

RANGE

TO DINING AREA →

SINK

D/W

In place of a wall that separated the kitchen and dining areas, the owners installed a custom-made steel breakfast bar-cum-backsplash they designed themselves. The countertops are black walnut.

the new kitchen to reflect their "industrial eclectic" taste, as Kelton characterizes it. And like many couples who entertain, they didn't want to be separated from guests while cooking dinner.

SOLUTION
Kelton's original budget allotted $4,500 for appliances and fixtures and $1,500 for cabinets—although he hadn't figured out what he could afford for that amount. That left $1,000 to cover the work he couldn't do himself.

He wanted to make one major structural change: eliminating the non-load-bearing wall separating the kitchen and dining rooms. So Kelton invited his parents and some friends to help demolish it. But some work had to be farmed out. A plumber moved the gas line several feet across the room to accommodate a new range with a built-in downdraft vent, and he installed ducts under the floor to carry smoke and fumes out of the house. An electrician put in additional outlets, including one for the range. Then Kelton had the walls skimcoated. The cost of these three jobs was about $800.

Kelton then discovered that even the least expensive stock cabinets in wood would cost more than $5,000. He turned to a firm in Denver that sells salvaged kitchen cabinets. "They had a bunch of 1950s enameled steel ones from an apartment building," Kelton recalls. Total cost: $90. He had them sandblasted to expose the steel (cost: $120), then sealed them with a clear, matte-finish acrylic.

The dimensions of the recycled cabinets, as well as a steel file cabinet placed next to the range for storage, helped dictate the remaining fixtures. Once all the cabinets were positioned, Kelton hired a friend to build a multipurpose unit next to the dishwasher, using Baltic birch plywood. It includes open shelving, wood cubbies, and a wine rack. He also had a storage unit built above the fridge.

FINISHING TOUCHES
A local metalworking firm made the breakfast bar out of cold-pressed steel. "Steel can be used in a kitchen in many forms," says Steve Thomas. "And people don't realize how inexpensive it is to have a piece custom-made." The kitchen bar cost only $250, a small fraction of the price to fabricate a similar piece in granite or maple. It was just one more way to turn challenge into opportunity.

SPACE SAVERS
"A small kitchen forces you to be inventive, which can often lead to some cool solutions to storage problems."
— STEVE THOMAS

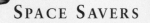

CLOCKWISE FROM ABOVE: 1. Hard-to-stack pot lids can be brought under control with a pot lid holder. 2. Knives are within easy reach on a magnet bar, which can be attached to a wall or cabinet. 3. A portable chrome shelf offers a quick way to double storage capacity. 4. Using vertical surfaces is one way to squeeze the most out of a compact work space. 5. With a tiered cookware stand, pots won't get lost in lower drawers.

From Knotty To Nice

A $12,000 kitchen makeover took energy, enthusiasm, elbow grease—and no fixed schedule

Hal Dantzler is a thrifty sort—not one to gut a kitchen when an update is all that is called for. He's also hardworking: In the year and a half since he and partner Anthony Alvarez bought this 1949 ranch house in Dallas, they've steadily remodeled the place in their spare time, starting with the kitchen. Because of budget restrictions, they did most of the work themselves, working at a pace that wouldn't inconvenience them. "I wouldn't recommend this approach to everyone," says Steve Thomas, "but for enthusiastic homeowners who have design ability and patience, taking on a project they can complete in a piecemeal fashion can pay off."

PROBLEM

At the time the house was purchased, the kitchen, though generous in size at 18 by 13 feet, was almost intolerably dreary. A pair of undersize corner windows provided the only natural

The low brick wall next to the range (ABOVE) was removed during the general demolition work. The new fireplace area (RIGHT) now has a strong connection to the kitchen.

illumination. Dark-stained, knotty-pine paneling and cabinetry and indoor-outdoor carpet absorbed all the light. The white refrigerator stood out against the gloom and, almost inevitably, became the focal point of the room.

SOLUTION

Dantzler began the job by replacing the corner windows with new thermal-pane, double-hung models, then added two more alongside. To do this, the men removed wall cabinets, then hired a contractor to cut the opening and install the windows. "They knew what to leave to the pros," Steve says.

Because the remaining cabinets were well built, Dantzler opted to keep them. Semigloss white paint cheers them considerably. "The all-white scheme was an antidote to the darkness," says Dantzler. To keep costs down, the existing black-iron hardware was supplemented with a few coordinated knobs.

An alcove for a new refrigerator was created by claiming the closet of a bedroom that became an entryway. To fill in the spot where the refrigerator had been, Dantzler, recycling pieces from the cabinetry removed earlier, created a base cabinet to house the microwave. Above it, he hung a glass-fronted, unfinished pine cupboard from a home-supply store. Both pieces were painted white to match the rest of the cabinetry in the room.

The range, a commercial model bought at auction, emits an enormous amount of heat and requires plenty of clearance. So for safety reasons it stands alone, is backed by (and rests on) tiles, and has a powerful hood.

FINISHING TOUCHES

The men lucked out when they ripped up the carpeting. Underneath was linoleum—but below that they discovered pine floorboards, which Dantzler painted a greenish teal with a high-gloss finish. "If I get tired of it, I can always repaint it," he says. Ambient lighting in the room is supplied by recessed halogen spots, which replaced Tiffany-style hanging lamps.

"To give yourself a new kitchen for $12,000," says Steve, "is really quite amazing. But, as this project proves, with imagination, you can achieve a lot for very little."

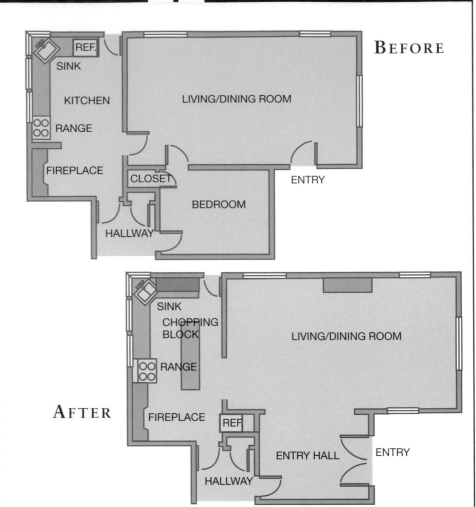

The new bank of windows that wraps around the corner sink bathes it in natural light. Pendant lights hang above.

Gourmet Nook

A 100-square-foot kitchen is outfitted with everything its owner asked for, including a grand restaurant-quality range

IN A WAY, THE DESIGN—OR LACK OF IT—MADE a remodel of Richard Schwartz's old kitchen easy. There was nothing to be done but to gut it. The 10-foot by 10-foot space consisted—in its entirety—of one metal wall cabinet, a sink in a detached cabinet, and a stove from the 1950s. It didn't even have a refrigerator. And the single window faced an air shaft. Schwartz, a professor at the City University of New York Graduate Center, bought the Brooklyn Heights apartment at the urging of his friends and former neighbors, architects Vicky and Richard Cameron. "The building is very friendly, with a very 'community' feeling, and the apartment was a good deal," he recalls. "I liked its layout and loved the 13-foot-high ceilings and architectural moldings, but it was in bad shape," he adds. "The Camerons told me they could make it great."

PROBLEM

Schwartz, a gourmet cook, knew exactly what he wanted: a restaurant-quality range, a refrigerator, and a wine rack. He knew space would be an issue and his budget for the job—$30,000—was tight by New York City standards. He told the architects they could skimp on everything else in order to outfit the kitchen with the equipment he desired. "This is a tight kitchen, so fitting in all the machines an avid cook needs demanded a great deal of organization," says Steve Thomas.

As for style, Schwartz asked for the hominess of an Italian country kitchen. Because he didn't want the expense and inconvenience of having to rent a place while the work was being done, the Camerons, along with their partner, Andy Taylor, had to complete the kitchen (as well as other parts of the apartment) during the six-month period that Schwartz was on sabbatical in California.

Lever handles and a rotating faucet accent the new, stainless-steel double-bowl sink. All cabinet knobs and bin pulls are reproductions.

BEFORE

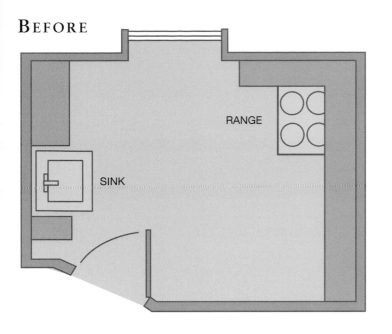

RANGE

SINK

AFTER

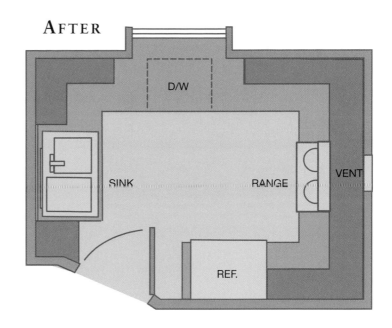

D/W

SINK   RANGE   VENT

REF.

SOLUTION

"Most cooks would pale at the thought of creating full meals in such a small space," says Steve of Schwartz's 100-square-foot kitchen. "From a design perspective," he adds, "it means you have to make the most of every square inch." The architects did just that by devoting the bulk of the real estate to the range and refrigerator-then organizing the cabinetry, open shelves, and countertops around them. "There was no room for a table or an island, but there was just enough to shoehorn a wine rack in next to the sink," says Steve. "It's a very efficient kitchen, like a galley on a boat; you just have to be sure that the friends you are cooking with know where you're headed with a hot sauté pan!"

After demolition, electrical work, and plumbing, the bulk of the budget went to the range and refrigerator, which meant the architects had little to spend on cabinetry. Although they were originally going to use stock units, their contractor said that since the job required so few cabinets, he could custom-make them in his shop-—from birch-veneer plywood with poplar rails and stiles, primed and painted—for about the same price. Wall cabinets were faced with glass doors; to shave costs, the architects opted for single panes of glass rather than divided lights.

The fact that the kitchen looked out onto an air shaft proved to be a blessing in disguise. When it came time to vent the hood required by the range, the architects found that restrictions on altering

In the new kitchen (LEFT), each cabinet was given a very specific function: to store dishes, foods, or 21 wine bottles (ABOVE).

the exterior of the 100-year-old apartment building didn't apply to the air shaft, so they could tunnel a vent through the range wall to the outside without worrying that the co-op's board of directors might reject their plan.

FINISHING TOUCHES

The window doesn't look out on any vineyards, so the architects brought in the charm of Italy with decorative tiles depicting pastoral scenes, which were inlaid within fields of yellow tiles set on the diagonal and framed by textural "spacers." These "pictures," in turn, were dropped into a traditional, plain white ceramic backsplash. "In a room with no natural light, you need places for the eye to rest," says Steve. The floor is covered with 6-inch-square handmade terra-cotta tiles; these were installed bottomside up to highlight their rustic nature, and then sealed several times to withstand any spills. The blue-toned countertop, made of a high-density silicate known as Pietra di Cardoso, echoes the blue of the inset tiles. The silicate marries the durability of granite with the beauty of soapstone.

The chrome reproduction hardware (and the ceiling lighting fixture) came from home-products catalogs; the hardware and fixture fit into the scheme perfectly. And, they were inexpensive, too. "For a mini-country kitchen," says Steve, "this one feels big. And, in the end, that's no small feat."

Thorougly Modern Makeover

The update of a '60s-era kitchen increases the room's efficiency while retaining its period flavor

THESE DAYS, WHEN SO MANY PEOPLE choose to transform or tear down postwar houses, the owners of this split-level in Chevy Chase, Maryland, bucked the trend. After almost 25 years in residence, they knew their kitchen had to be updated, but they wanted it to fit the rest of the house. They found a kindred spirit in architect Dean Brenneman, of Washington, D.C., who respected their wish and told them he'd make it look "as if it were done by the original architect—on his best day and with a good budget."

The homeowners, both doctors, had longed to modernize the kitchen. But, like many busy couples juggling career and family responsibilities, they didn't get around to the project until their children moved out. "It makes sense," says Steve Thomas. "Raising kids is such a full-time job that most people can't imagine going through a six-month renovation—especially one that puts the heart of the house out of commission. "

PROBLEM

The old kitchen was gloomy, illuminated by one small window, and burdened with overbearing dark wood beams and trim. Plastic laminate made to resemble Delft tile had been grafted onto the cabinetry in a misguided attempt to bring color and pattern into the room. The layout was awkward as well: Two doors opened into the space and a third led outdoors, turning the room into a thoroughfare.

The wife, who loves to cook, had a very clear wish list. "I wanted an island because I needed extra counter space," she recalls, "and two dishwashers because I enjoy entertaining but don't like cleanup, and a professional gas range for flexibility."

SOLUTION

To create enough space for a separate breakfast area, Brenneman pushed the rear wall back 8½ feet—the maximum allowed

ABOVE: The old kitchen had long served the family's needs, but once the couple became empty-nesters, they found it awkward and impractical for entertaining. RIGHT: The new kitchen was enlarged to include an airy and expansive eating area and a bar that includes a wine cooler.

by local zoning. He also angled that wall to follow the property's idiosyncratic lot line. The angle opened up space for a large window with an expansive view of the garden. Sliding doors replaced the old window and back door. The angle of the wall also echoes that of the gently pitched ceiling, a detail the couple decided to retain.

This new breakfast area doubles as a gathering spot for drinks with friends. Nearby are a side-by-side refrigerator/freezer, a wine cooler, and a bar-size sink in the island. "This is an excellent layout," says Steve, "You've got a cook's area, a food-prep area

ABOVE: Pot storage and warming drawers near the cooktop prove exceptionally useful and convenient.

at the sink, a prep area at the island, and a hanging-out space where you can chat with the cook."

The black-and-blond color scheme was inspired by visits to an art museum. Glossy black granite countertops and wall ovens with black glass doors stand out in sharp contrast to the red-birch cabinets. To unify the various zones within the space, Brenneman covered the floor with 12-inch-square terra-cotta tiles.

Architect Brenneman prefers custom over semicustom cabinets. "When you're renovating a house, the walls are never smooth and the floors are never level," he explains. "You've got to make pre-fabricated components fit, which involves extra labor. We've found that semi-custom is really no cheaper." Because she is short and didn't want to have to haul out a step stool to reach the top shelves, the wife requested that the wall cabinets be hung at a lower than normal height.

Brenneman chose professional-quality appliances clad in stainless steel, including a pair of warming drawers installed under the cooktop. Nearby are a pair of stacking wall ovens and a microwave, plus a garage for small appliances.

FINISHING TOUCHES
Upgrading the lighting from the old rectangular fluorescent fixture was tricky. "Because we left the original ceiling alone and this part of the house is only one story," says Brenneman, "we couldn't rewire easily." His solution: mono-point fixtures installed on mounting plates, plus task lighting beneath the wall cabinets.

Today the kitchen blends seamlessly with the rest of the house. When the couple had 24 people over for Thanksgiving, the kitchen made it easy.

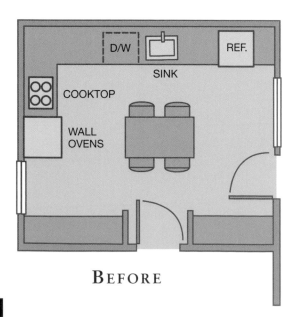

BEFORE

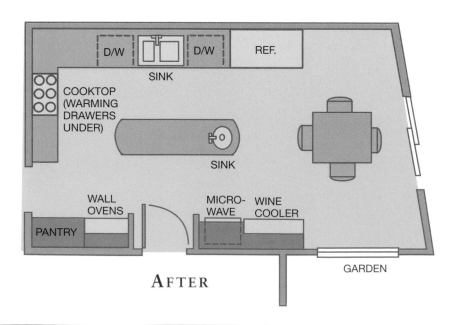

AFTER

Canadian Maple

Pale, clean-lined cabinetry highlights a kitchen update

ABOVE: **Light maple cabinets are an upgrade from the dark veneered-oak cabinets (LEFT) that were installed at the time the house was built.**

ACCORDING TO THE NATIONAL KITCHEN and Bath Association, the cost of a kitchen renovation these days averages about $27,000, which makes Canadian pharmacist—and longtime *This Old House* fan—Eugene Baron's remodeling price tag of under $17,000 more than just a little impressive. "This is a kitchen on an unbelievable budget," says host Steve Thomas admiringly. "Luckily, Eugene already had a good bit of building experience, so he could do some parts of the work himself."

Woodworking has been a lifelong hobby for Baron—ever since he was encouraged to build a cabinet from scratch to showcase his prized rock collection in an eighth-grade shop class. For years he contented himself with relatively modest improvement projects on the single-story bunga-low, built in 1971, that he shares with Gwen Satran. He was particularly proud of the table he made that perfectly fit the alcove in their kitchen.

But five years ago, Baron felt ready to progress beyond the table, and he decided to tackle a remodel of the entire room. A pharmacist's salary would go only so far, but he figured he would avoid excessive labor costs if he did part of the work, such as demolition, himself. To further off-set expenses, the couple received an unexpected tax rebate: Their home city of Winnipeg offered

All new cabinetry was installed, adding additional storage and workspace above and to the right of the microwave and range. Maple bullnose trim accents the stone-look laminate countertops.

$1,500 ($500 a year over a three-year period) to homeowners who made capital improvements to qualified dwellings over 25 years old that were appraised for less than $100,000. The kitchen pro-ject fit both criteria.

PROBLEM
Except for a pantry closet constructed by Baron and a recently purchased range and refrigerator, the kitchen had remained untouched since the house was built. With a tile-patterned, tan-and-gold linoleum floor and ugly oak-veneered particleboard cabinets, the room looked its age. The breakfast nook featured a large, square, shuttered interior window that took in a view of the entry hall and front door. And the dishwasher couldn't be opened at the same time as the cabinet it adjoined.

SOLUTION

Gwen and Eugene visited more than a dozen show-rooms but couldn't find cabinets that satisfied both their aesthetic and price requirements. Then they hired a designer . . . whose solution didn't please them. Finally, in 1998, they stopped in at a local kitchen showroom. The couple liked the clean-lined cabinetry there, and they felt an instant rap-port with the company's owner and resident designer, Alan Cheung. "Even though Eugene and Gwen had a tight budget, they took the right first step," says Steve. "They enlisted design expertise."

"Cheung faced a daunting task," he adds. "He couldn't move the plumbing, nor could he increase the footprint." Considering his options (or lack of them), Cheung decided to focus on maximizing the available space. He first recommended that Baron fill in the interior window in the eating area so it would feel more private. His next suggestion—to remove a wall and pocket door between the nook and a side hall—not only improved traffic flow throughout the kitchen but also offered easier access to a home office across the hall. As a bonus, the new opening allowed Baron to add a set of cab-inets, with countertop, to the right of the range. The stove and refrigerator were still serviceable, so they stayed put; a new dishwasher was relocat-ed to the end of a perpendicular cabinet run.

Once Baron removed the old flooring and

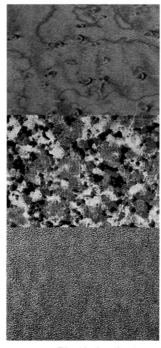

FROM TOP: Plastic laminate isn't always the first choice for countertops these days, but it offers good value, as well as a huge selection of colors and patterns.

replaced the subfloor, Cheung's crew came in and installed the custom maple cabinets. Because they were so well made, Baron allotted almost two-thirds of his budget for these. "Eugene made a good decision here," Steve says. "Light-colored maple helps enlarge the space visually. Dark-stained oak, like they had before, would have made the room feel much smaller."

OVERCOMING THE OBSTACLES

Baron's project had its share of aggravations. After removing the wall between the nook and hall, he discovered that it had been load-bearing. "The dry-waller was to come the next day, so I had to work until 2 a.m. installing a new 2x10 joist and sister-ing 2x4 posts to support the opening."

What turned out to be the toughest chore was installing the built-in microwave over the range, though it should have been one of the easiest. "A friend and I had to take out a medicine cabinet in the bathroom behind, put in a sheet of $\frac{5}{8}$-inch ply-wood, attach a mounting plate to the plywood, then remount the cabinet—all before hanging the microwave," Baron says. "An hour-long job wound up taking five." Was the effort worth it? Baron says he knew it was when his wife's uncle came to visit. As he watched her show off the kitchen, he listened to the pride in her voice, and he could only smile.

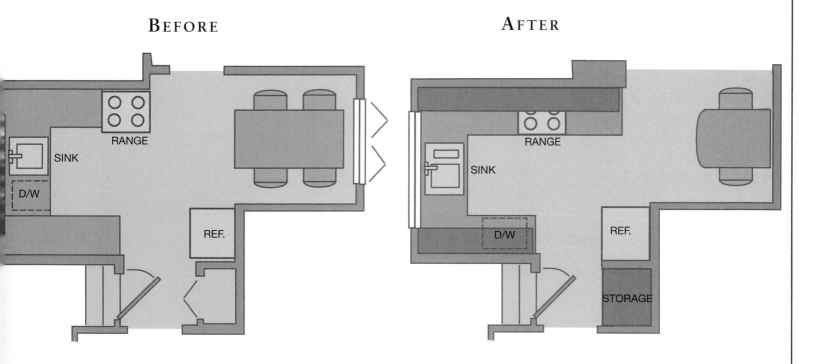

BEFORE

AFTER

A Silvery Lining

In a turn-of-the-century bungalow, this kitchen is carefully planned—and outfitted—to look casual

BUYING A RUNDOWN 1898 Arts and Crafts–style bungalow in Coronado, California, was, Patricia DiCicco's family insisted, a supreme act of folly. But DiCicco always loved old houses, and she fell for this one right away. "Most people considered the place a teardown," she says, "But I saw its potential." DiCicco's passion was not lost on Steve Thomas. "I grew up in a bungalow in Berkeley, and there's something about that style that epitomizes home," he says.

Coronado is a long-established resort community on a peninsula between San Diego Bay and the Pacific Ocean. For DiCicco, whose main home is in Palo Alto, the town looked like the ideal spot for her and her husband's retirement. Until that time came, they and their sons could use the bungalow now and then as a weekend getaway; she also hoped to rent it out for the summer.

A born optimist, DiCicco bought the house in December 1998. Big tasks included a complete rewiring and replumbing. And then there was the kitchen.

RIGHT: **Patricia DiCicco surveys her new kitchen.**
ABOVE: **A peninsula cut the old kitchen in two.**

PROBLEM

The kitchen suffered from misguided—and cheap—attempts at modernization. "It was so depressing," says DiCicco. When previous homeowners added bathrooms on the second floor, they simply snaked the plumbing lines above the windows over the kitchen sink and boxed them in behind 18-inch-high soffits. When they needed more cupboards, they stuck them in willy-nilly. A skimpy peninsula bisected the 12-by-20-foot room, and three layers of linoleum covered the floors.

While all this clearly needed fixing, DiCicco decided she'd rather live with the kitchen's inconvenient location—it connects the house to the backyard—than alter the footprint of the house.

ABOVE: Wall cabinets were installed without soffits to align with existing windows. RIGHT: A second-hand refrigerator and range with hood saved more than two-thirds of what they would have cost new.

SOLUTION

To ready the room for its facelift, DiCicco gutted it. The demolition revealed that the Douglas-fir floor—which ran in three different directions beneath the linoleum— couldn't be salvaged. DiCicco chose a high-pressure wood-look laminate to replace it: "I wanted a floor I wouldn't have to worry about with renters or my kids."

DiCicco designed the new kitchen as a modern version of the so-called unfitted kitchens authentic to the Arts and Crafts period. In those kitchens, layouts followed no plan and virtually every appliance and cabinet stood alone. In DiCicco's update, she ran lightly stained, Douglas-fir Shaker-style cabinets

A multipendant lamp branching from a single, centered stem helps to anchor the room.

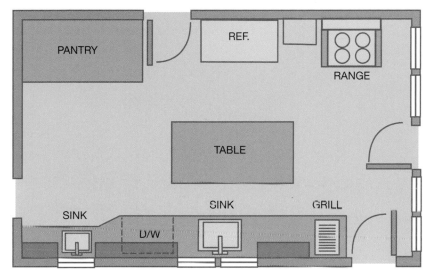

PANTRY

REF.

RANGE

TABLE

SINK

D/W

SINK

GRILL

only along the sink wall, and the sole built-in appliances are the dishwasher and a grill. The refrigerator and range stand independently, as does the table that centers the room. "A busy cook might find the layout frustrating," says Steve, "because you have to go around the table to get anywhere—but it serves this family's purposes." To make the arrangement more attractive to renters, DiCicco added a small second sink near the dishwasher to handle the extra glassware a family typically uses during the summer.

DiCicco had been searching for a 1940s-era stove when a friend back home offered her a second-hand commercial-grade refrigerator, range, and hood at a great price. Her husband rented a truck and drove them down.

FINISHING TOUCHES

To enhance the unfitted look and complement the stainless-steel appliances, DiCicco placed a 30-by-72-inch kitchen table with a stainless top in the center of the room; it takes the place of a traditional island. A Craftsman-inspired lighting fixture provides task lighting and overall illumination for dining. To display cookware, DiCicco bought movable wire shelving on wheels. For the countertops, she chose a stonelike porcelain tile. The backsplash is tumbled marble in a similar hue.

"The transformation of the kitchen—and the rest of the house—has made believers out of DiCicco's husband and sons, who've come to love the place as much as she does," says Steve.

LIGHTS THAT REINFORCE YOUR KITCHEN'S STYLE

In modern kitchens, the bare bulbs of yore are often replaced with single pendants—or a fixture with multiple pendants branching from a single stem. Branched units mount on a single electrical box, often an advantage.

1. This brushed-brass single-pole pendant has an opalescent shade; poles can be ordered in various lengths. 2. A somewhat larger pendant, this one can handle bulbs up to 150 watts. 3. A white painted metal framework supports the fluted glass shade of this retrofitted mid-century pendant.

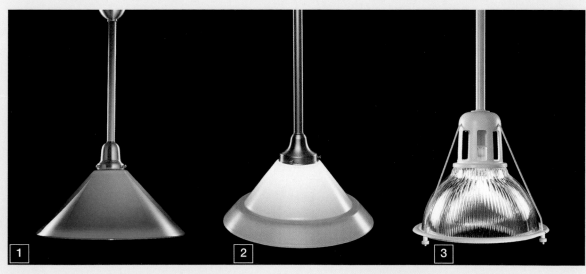

1

2

3

Pass-Through Kitchen

By eliminating a doorway and repositioning appliances, this modest kitchen accommodates traffic and a cook

DEBORAH ASHFORD BOUGHT HER RAMBLING 1909 Arts and Crafts-style house in Washington, D.C., because it was almost perfect. It was spacious enough to allow each of her four daughters—ranging in age from 6 to 19—a room of her own, and its out-of-the-hub location "feels like a village within a big city," she says. The area and the beauty of the house more than compensated for its eyesore of a kitchen. Ashford, a lawyer and a single mom, didn't like the room's spartan and inefficient design. But "a big, eat-in, 'heart of the home' kitchen doesn't mean anything to me," she says. "I'm rarely in it." Her goal wasn't to turn the room into a gourmet showplace, just to create a pleasing, productive command station that could be utilized as effectively by the housekeeper as by her. "I like Deborah's honest approach," says Steve Thomas. "She had a small kitchen, and she worked with it."

PROBLEM

Asked to describe the old kitchen, Ashford says, "It was essentially a hallway with appliances in it." Three doors opened into the 10-by-11-foot space, and everyone cut through it on their way to the family room. The positioning of the doors allowed only two spots for storage: a bank of base cabinets flanking a sink under, and a hutch-style cupboard standing across from a '50s-era stove. Worse, the family room, a recent addition, had robbed the kitchen of its pantry, leaving Ashford with no place to stock provisions.

Redirecting the traffic and reorganizing the work zones were just two of the directives Ashford passed along to local architect Norman Smith and his wife, contractor Gail Montplaisir. She also wanted the room to blend aesthetically with the rest of her Craftsman-style home, and she had a tight budget. "Having a designer and contractor who work closely together makes for a more streamlined building process," says Steve.

ABOVE: The former kitchen had no focus and few amenities. RIGHT: In the redesign, food prep is cosolidated on one side of the room, liberating the rest of the space to provide a passage to the family room from a hall and dining room.

SOLUTION

To aid circulation and create a viable work triangle, Smith decided to deflect traffic by closing off the door that linked the

cooking area to an adjacent hallway while leaving the other two doors intact. "Once we did that, the space lent itself to a U-shaped plan, with a passage across the open end," he explains. Next, he pushed back the wall that separated the kitchen from the hall to gain 4 precious inches of floor space. Four inches may not seem like a lot, but the extra depth meant Smith could reframe a 10-foot section of wall to accommodate a bank of cabinets surrounding a new sink.

Another architectural detail, and one that gives the illusion of greater space, is a reverse soffit: Smith dropped the ceiling at the perimeter of the room, without building up the cabinetry to meet it. His strategy solved two problems: It gave him a place to recess down lights without bumping into any joists, and it keeps the room from looking too boxy. "If we'd taken the cabinetry all the way up to the ceiling, the room would have appeared even smaller," Smith says.

As a budget measure, Smith chose ready-made carcasses for most of the cabinets, to which he added specially designed, furniture-grade oak-plywood doors and drawers. To evoke the Arts and Crafts style in the rest of the house, the architect affixed narrow strips of oak over the undivided panes of glass on the glazed cabinet doors, then attached simple sawn-oak pulls, of

The backs of the upper cabinets were glassed in to bring light in from the study across the hall.

BEFORE

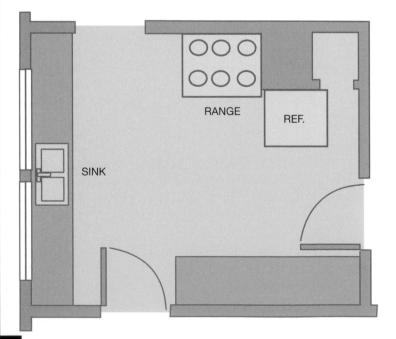

AFTER

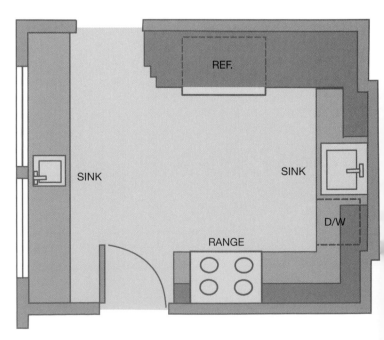

SPEED DEMONS

"In a small kitchen, the more you can build in, the bigger the space will seem. Microwaves and newer fast-cookers fit the bill because they take up less wall space than conventional ovens."

— STEVE THOMAS

Using light as the energy source, this 30-inch-wide, high-speed wall oven can bake, broil, grill, and even roast foods up to eight times faster than a conventional oven. The unit can also serve as a 950-watt microwave oven.

A chicken can be prepared in less than 10 minutes in this 24-inch-wide convection steam oven. The three-shelf unit, which requires no plumbing, uses a refillable water reservoir to supply the steam.

This 27- or 30-inch-wide convection/micro-wave high-speed wall oven can be installed as a single unit or paired with a standard convection oven.

The stainless-steel backsplash visually links the counters with the stainless-steel appliances.

his own design, with stainless-steel pan-head screws. The floor, original to the room, is quartersawn pine.

FINISHING TOUCHES

Green tile on the countertops pays tribute to the home's origins: The color is found frequently in art pottery of the Arts and Crafts period. In contrast, the stainless-steel backsplash and appliances look thoroughly modern. Since Ashford doesn't consider herself a gourmet cook, she settled for a residential version of a commercial range, with a microwave and vent above. "If you don't cook a whole lot, you don't need a really big hood," says Steve. "Your equipment should always be matched to your cooking style."

"The details in this kitchen, like the oak and the glass, are materials that are representative of Craftsman-style houses," he adds. "One of the founding principles of this movement was to let materials speak for themselves—not try to disguise them as something else. That's what Norman has done here. Everything speaks in its own voice." To which Ashford and her four daughters chorus an appreciative "Yes!"

Key West, Italian Style

An open kitchen was enclosed, then fitted with sleek imported cabinets for a dose of *la dolce vita*

THE MORNING SUN BLAZED ABOVE KEY WEST, FLORIDA, as Michael Miller surveyed his cluttered back porch. For weeks the porch had served as a staging area for the renovation of Miller's 19th-century conch cottage, *This Old House*'s winter project house. But on this day, tools and equipment had been shunted aside to make room for Miller's new kitchen: 25 cardboard boxes containing parts for 18 Italian-made modular components. Miller shook his head, relieved that he didn't have to take this on. John Mele and Mike Speer, installers dispatched from the manufacturer's Manhattan showroom, were already unpacking their tools.

Paging through a European kitchen catalog, Miller and his wife, Helen Colley, were intrigued by the combination of cherrywood veneer, stainless steel, and glass cabinetry that characterized the company's wares. The warm but ultra-streamlined look radiated that quintessential Italian sensibility—*la dolce vita* (the good life)—and seemed perfect fit for the balmy, laid-back Keys.

PROBLEM

When Miller and Colley bought their property, they knew they wanted to get rid of the open kitchen because it blocked the view of the backyard. There was a more practical reason as well. "I wanted an enclosed kitchen because I didn't want to be able to see dirty dishes from the living room," says Colley.

ABOVE: The cherry-veneer cabinets feature flush doors and drawers.
RIGHT: Sleek surfaces include granite floor tiles and granite countertops.

SOLUTION

To achieve her goal, the couple converted a side porch into a galley-shaped space, complete with a casement window over the sink, French doors leading onto the back porch, and niches for major appliances. They also closed up a porch on the other side of the house to create a dining area. A lantern-ceilinged great room took up the center.

With the rough spaces carved out, it was time to fit the

kitchen. As Mele and Speer pulled a cabinet with frosted-glass drawers out of a box, Colley looked impressed. "Mmm," she said. "It is beautiful. What do you think, Managua?" The couple's honey-colored German shepherd-Chow sniffed and then licked the glass. Mele wiped away the drool. "Oh, well," said Colley. "At least glass is easy to clean."

Under the cabinets' handsome facade was a carefully engineered system of hardware. Instead of being screwed into the wall, the uppers were hung on a slender aluminum bar, then raised or lowered with a leveling device mounted inside. Lower cabinets were supported by legs that can be adjusted up or down as duty calls. Steve Thomas was especially taken with the way the cabinet drawer-fronts can be removed for easy cleaning and with the drawers' hidden gliding system. "No one ever needs to see those ugly tracks."

The company's Italian designers pride themselves on creating stylish, efficient kitchens in six basic styles. Although the components are

LEFT: A stainless-steel backsplash takes the heat—and splatters—from the indoor grill and dedicated wok burner. The latter can be converted to accomodate large pots. BELOW: One sink is outfitted with an old-fashioned gooseneck faucet and the other with a contemporary chrome sprayer to reflect the house's marriage of old and new styles. RIGHT: It was the glass-fronted drawers that helped convince Colley to order the kitchen from Italy.

modular, they can be custom-fitted to specific dimensions. Whereas Italians tend to respect the conceptual integrity behind a particular line and wouldn't dream of marrying one style with a different style, Americans think nothing of exercising their individualism by ordering elements à la carte and mixing different looks. Colley and Miller were no exception, choosing cherrywood drawers from one line, frosted-glass drawers from another, and thick, satin-stainless-steel sculptural handles from yet another. They added wireglass windows, a coral-granite countertop, and a floor composed of black granite tiles.

"Even though we have a traditional house, we thought this blend of styles was the right way to go," says Miller. "I thought, 'This is just good art.'"

And highly functional too. This kitchen makes it easy to whip up a feast and carry the food out to guests on the back porch. When an architect friend visits, he enjoys using the kitchen's built-in wok. With a 4½-foot-wide aisle, the kitchen allows all three of them to pull together a dinner without feeling cramped.

Installing the cabinets required the same precision as installing conventional cabinetry. The trickiest part was making sure that all the cabinets were perfectly aligned and properly fitted. With cabinets dimensioned to metric measurements, it took some effort—and some rebuilding of walls—to match them to a house measured out in inches.

He Cooks, She Cooks

A kitchen redo with an open plan provides an efficient and luxurious workspace for two cooks

Twenty years ago, when photographer Fran Brennan and her husband, Dan, bought their 1936 Colonial in Houston, Fran did all the cooking. Dan's culinary skills extended only as far as the traditional outdoor grill. But in the years since, Dan has become an accomplished amateur chef.

Unfortunately, the more time the Brennans spent preparing meals in the compact kitchen, the more they found themselves stepping on each other's toes.

PROBLEM

Creating a kitchen for two cooks is a challenge familiar to Steve Thomas. "Many couples—and even their kids—are cooking as a team now," he says. "So when they remodel, they often request areas tailored to their culinary specialties." The Brennans' demands were more basic. "The kitchen was so tiny, there was about two feet of counter space for each of us on either side of the sink, and only a little more on the island," says Fran. Their goal: to carve out independent prep areas.

There were other reasons to enlarge the kitchen. Before dinner parties, people would gather and watch Fran cook. "It drove me crazy," she admits.

RIGHT: The open-plan kitchen readily accommodates two cooks and eases traffic flow. ABOVE: Large-print wallpaper made the once-tight space feel even smaller.

SOLUTION

Houston architect David Feeback annexed the adjacent laundry area (relocating it upstairs) and tore out a rear wall to enlarge the house with a two-story bump-out extending 3 feet into the backyard. He eliminated the wall that separated the kitchen from Fran's study, turning that space into an eating area, which would open via French doors onto a patio. By eliminating the laundry/kitchen wall and the study/kitchen wall, Feeback was able to expand and reposition the kitchen island. Giving it a 90-degree turn allowed for one that measured 84 by 50 inches. To develop two separate work zones, Feeback focused on sink placement. He put a farmhouse-style sink beneath the window, in the middle of the now extended, wall-to-wall countertop. A smaller sink went in the corner of the island opposite the refrigerator.

With a pot rack suspended above the stove, cooking vapors are sucked through a downdraft system housed beneath the cooktop "Downdrafts are an key item in the tool kit for a designer of an open-plan kitchen," says Steve. For maximum efficiency, he says, "keep the duct run short and, when cooking, put the vapor-producing dishes on the burners closest to the vent."

To achieve the French country look, new custom poplar cabinets were painted a taupe-gray and sanded in some areas for an antique finish. A pantry closet by the back door provides needed storage, as does a floor-to-ceiling cabinet for china and silver that's within easy reach of the dishwasher.

Fran specified concrete countertops. "I like concrete's color and texture," she says. Because concrete is very porous, says Feeback, the countertop was sealed before installation and must be resealed periodically. "Concrete counters can be coated with carnauba wax for protection, just like a car," says Steve. "But if you covet a pristine counter, forget concrete. They're for people who like the weathered look of a beat-up leather jacket."

Says Fran: "My husband keeps saying how much he loves our whole house thanks to the new kitchen." Now, says Steve, the Brennans no longer need to dance a tortured tango: "They can finally cook comfortably together."

ABOVE: The kitchen now boasts a large, airy kitchen that includes a practical island workstation and an inviting eating area. RIGHT: The cooktop is ventilated via a downdraft unit, which raises up or lowers with the push of a button. A fan duct in the cabinet below pulls fumes and odors down and out of the house.

BEFORE

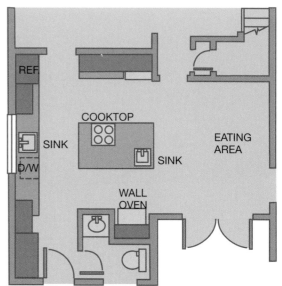

AFTER

Kitchen By the Sea

A new kitchen for a beach house: clean lines and cleanable materials

A square cubby below the countertop adds visual interest by breaking up the expanse of light wood, making a perfect spot to stash a foaming cup for the cappuccino maker.

A PARTNER IN THE BUSY NEW YORK City architecture firm of Sidnam Petrone Gartner, Coty Sidnam needs a break every now and then. Luckily, she has a way to get one: a house on Fire Island, the car-free, carefree, 32-mile-long sandspit that stretches along the south shore of Long Island. "We rented for a while, but about four years ago we decided to make it permanent," says Sidnam, speaking for her husband, Derek Huntington, and their three children. "Coming out here keeps us sane."

First built in the 1920s, the three-bedroom bungalow the family settled on is among numerous houses destroyed in the hurricane of 1938, then reconstructed by the original builder from salvaged materials. The two-story shingled cottage is rustic yet playful, with its battened walls painted a range of pastels—very much in keeping with the beach house sensibility. "This house isn't elegant," says Sidnam. "Its candy colors and simplicity make it feel more like an ice cream parlor."

PROBLEM

Having designed some 50 kitchens, Sidnam is used to the finest materials and latest appliances. But when it came to her own 54-square-foot kitchen, she didn't mind fake terra-cotta floor tile, gold-flecked Formica countertops, plain pine cabinets, or even the "classic 1959" refrigerator with its broken seal and rusted-out grille. Eventually, however, the fussy electric stove and the lack of storage space got old. The owner of a compact island retreat himself, Steve Thomas can relate. "When your house is somewhat remote, you want to stock up on everything from paper towels to canned artichokes," says Steve. "And you need plenty of room to store them." Sidnam decided to apply her problem-solving expertise to her own situation. Her goal was a kitchen that looked modern yet not industrial and that maximized the existing space.

LEFT: The old, nondescript cabinets wasted valuable storage space on top. ABOVE: Blond wood is accented with "beach" glass to make this cozy kitchen feel more spacious. RIGHT: Pairs of drawer and cabinet pulls are set in different directions, but not for any special reason—it's just for fun.

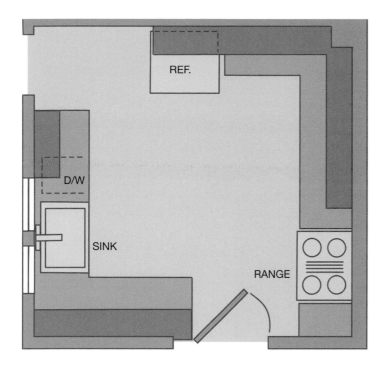

SOLUTION

After a few sketches, Sidnam realized she couldn't reorganize the layout without significantly changing the footprint—something she didn't want to attempt. She liked the way the kitchen functioned as a passageway connecting the mudroom and dining room. So rather than tear down walls and rearrange the space, she kept things pretty much where they were, making mostly nonstructural changes, such as putting in new cabinets, flooring, counters, and appliances.

The kitchen did wind up undergoing some minor construction. Fire Island contractor Ken Larson moved part of a wall back 3 feet, giving the not-quite-square room a more regular shape, and adding 40 square feet by absorbing a guest room closet. ("Guests don't need to hang up clothes—they'll stay too long," Sidnam says jokingly.) Sidnam hung battens to match those throughout the house, then painted the room a "beachy" aqua blue.

During the renovation, Larson uncovered slapdash work by previous owners. Ripping up the flooring, he found "tile on top of linoleum, on top of vinyl—a real mess," he says. And when he went to replace the sticky double-hung windows with larger ones, the header was missing. "The house hadn't fallen down without it, but a header is pretty essential," says Steve. "Installing one was easy and will help the house withstand hurricanes."

FINISHING TOUCHES

Construction work done, Sidnam searched for "graphic" materials to match her vivid house: stainless-steel appliances and custom beech and maple cabinets with blue- and blue-green-glass doors. "The glass is in keeping with the airiness of the house," says Steve. "And it adds sparkle and liveliness to the room." Sidnam considered opaque glass, but nixed the idea. "The clear stuff means I don't have to serve my kids and my houseguests. They can find their own plates without searching every cabinet." She chose a bold gray-blue limestone tile for the floor, and a dove-gray Corian for the counters, thinking granite or marble would be too formal for a beach house. She topped off the room with an industrial-style halogen hanging lamp in the center of the space, and small recessed lights built into the cabinets, and above the sink and stove. "In the end," says Steve, "Sidnam got not only a great kitchen but a wonderful showroom, too. I'm sure her clients on Fire Island will be inspired."

Saving The Ranch

A new kitchen is the key to the makeover of a 1950s suburban classic

WHILE LAURIE LEITNER LOVED THE PRIVACY OF her white-pine-filled yard in northern New Jersey, her house enthralled her considerably less: The brick-faced raised ranch had been built in the 1950s, and although roomy, it lacked a certain flair. "Make that total flair," says Leitner. The gray metal cabinets in the kitchen, for example, "looked like they belonged in a diner." But it wasn't just a problem with decor. Leitner and her husband have three children between the ages of 5 and 13 and craved such amenities as a family room, an eat-in kitchen, and a master bedroom suite.

Sitting down with an architect one spring, Leitner mentioned that she wanted "something prettier" in a house, while her husband wanted to make sure whatever they did was "not too flashy." For his part, the architect, Bill Kaufman of Wesketch Architecture in Liberty Corner, New Jersey, wanted to make sure the renovated house would blend in with the neighborhood. But like a domino chain, the renovation spread from room to room. Says Leitner, "Once we started fixing some things, we decided to fix everything." After eight months of work, the house grew from 3,200 to about 5,000 square feet. But it still nestles comfortably on top of the original foundation.

PROBLEM

Radical as it is, the project didn't begin as a whole-house makeover. The couple set out to simply spruce up the kitchen and add a family room. But, because the backyard sloped up a steep hill, "we couldn't just put on an addition with a master suite above and be done," says Leitner. That would have destroyed the park-like setting, the very thing they liked most about the place.

SOLUTION

As with many whole-house renovations, an entire team of design professionals—in addition to the architect—became necessary. The Leitners turned to interior designer Frank DelleDonne, of Summit, New Jersey, to take charge of the house's finishes, materials and furnishings, and hired Joan Picone of European Country

LEFT: The renovated 400-square-foot kitchen, which adjoins a 400-square-foot family room (ABOVE), displays antique-white glazed cabinets topped by crown molding repeated throughout the house. A dark-stained cherry island contains the sink and dishwasher. Beneath it all, the floor is covered with travertine marble cut into 18-inch squares—just the right scale for a space this size.
BELOW: To cut down on the jet-enginelike sound emanating from the vent hood, the builders installed the fan in the attic, rather than attaching it to the hood itself.

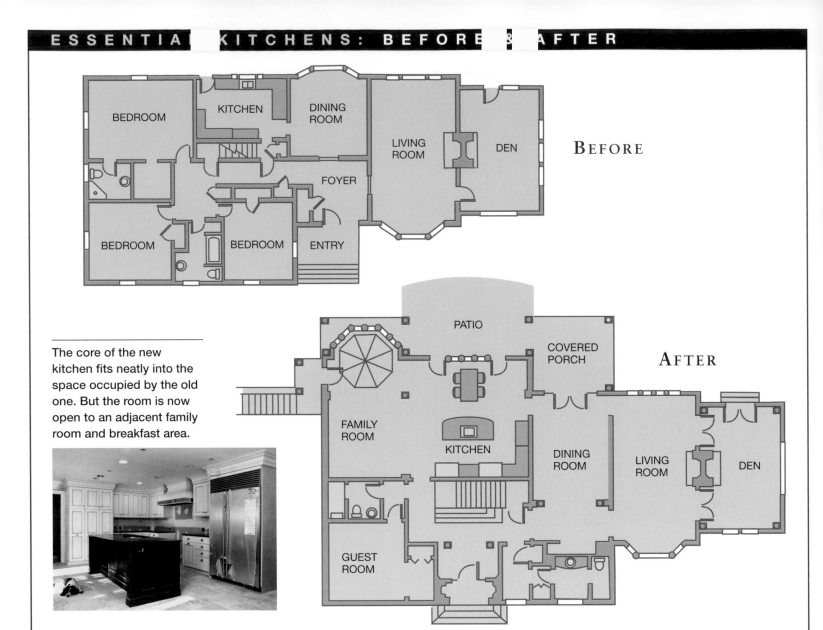

BEFORE

AFTER

The core of the new kitchen fits neatly into the space occupied by the old one. But the room is now open to an adjacent family room and breakfast area.

Kitchens in Far Hills, to design the kitchen. Designers can be pricey. Someone like DelleDonne charges between $10,000 and $30,000 to pick out bathroom tiles and wall colors and shop for furniture for a house this size. For her part, Picone charged a lawyerly $175 an hour to plan the kitchen. "We spare homeowners a lot of headaches," says DelleDonne. Leitner calls the two indispensable. "Without them," she says, "I really would have gone mad."

Besides planning how each room will look, DelleDonne made sure that the look carries over from room to room. This subtle uniformity can be seen in the pale-white travertine marble on the kitchen floor and the limestone of a similar color in the lavatory, as well as the antique-white glazed terra-cotta tile in the downstairs guest bathroom. "The goal is to have the interior design of the house act as a subtle reflection of the exterior architecture," says DelleDonne.

FINISHING DETAILS

To add a touch of elegance to the Leitner house, architect Bill Kaufman leaned on an ancient Greek tradition by adding classical columns. He chose the simplest design—a variation known as Tuscan—and used them liberally both inside and out. One pair made of ponderosa pine stand in the dining room, where they mark a passage to the living room and "define the table area as separate from the main walk," says Kaufman.

After eight long months of living in a rented house, Leitner and her family revel in their new surroundings. While Leitner takes charge of the marble-tiled kitchen, her children tune into the media center in the adjacent family room. "It's perfect," says Leitner, and all new—except for the white-painted mantelpiece in the living room, the only interior detail that survived the makeover. "I always liked it," says Leitner. And now, it reminds her of a house's remarkable journey.

Chef's Choice

For an exacting practitioner of the culinary arts, a well-organized kitchen is the recipe for success

ABOVE: One convenient feature of the new kitchen is the island sink, used for food prep and making drinks.

WITH A DEGREE FROM THE CULINARY Institute of America and nine years' experience testing recipes at a national food and wine magazine, the owner of this New Jersey kitchen had precise ideas about what she wanted when she and her husband undertook its remodeling.

Part of an ambitious revamping of their home, the kitchen was, not surprisingly, the wife's top priority. However, she harbored no desire for a high-glamour status symbol, nor did she want a gathering place for guests or family. Instead, she wanted a bright, attractive room that would function efficiently. "Everything she wanted is what a good cook demands," says Steve Thomas, "and that includes a gas cooktop and electric ovens. Gas offers more flexibility, and electricity, in ovens, maintains a consistent temperature."

PROBLEM

Cramped, and fitted out with knotty-pine cabinetry, the kitchen was like a museum—it had not been touched since the 1960s. The wife made do in the outmoded space for a year. "One

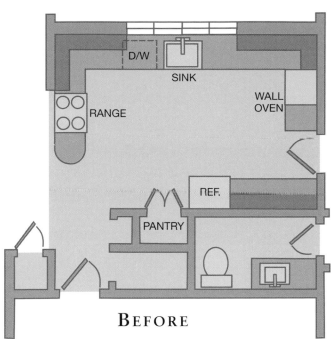

BEFORE

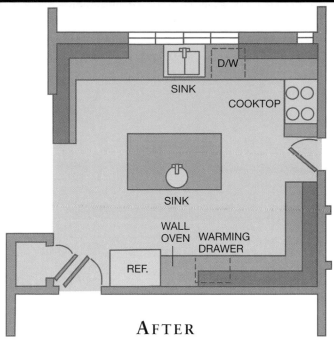

AFTER

of the things you learn as a chef is how to cook just about anywhere," she says.

Wish-list items specific to her level of expertise included professional-quality appliances and plenty of counter space near the double wall ovens and the cooktop, "so I could swing around with a hot pot and have a place to put it down right away." Because she entertains often, this cook also wanted a warming drawer. "It helps incredibly with timing," she says. "You can keep a dish warm and moist in there for up to two hours."

SOLUTION

Morristown, New Jersey–based architect Nick Bensley had remodeled the couple's previous home, and the couple knew him to be a listener. Right up front, Bensley came up with a way to expand the kitchen's footprint: Annex a powder room, pantry, and broom closet adjacent to a small lavatory. (He relocated the lavatory to a closet on the far side of the living room and moved the storage areas to a space near the laundry.) This maneuver freed up enough space to add a hefty 45-by-60-inch island. The unit, though, has no overhang to accommodate stools—the owner didn't want a kitchen that children would hang out in.

Knowing how much use the new cooktop would get, Bensley placed it in an outside corner of the room; here the stainless steel–lined hood could be easily vented outdoors. "For efficiency, you need a strong fan and a cooktop location that affords the shortest possible duct run," says Steve.

FINISHING TOUCHES

Countertops were made from deep-blue Italian

LEFT: Materials in the new kitchen create a light, cheerful ambience. In the old kitchen (INSET), dark cabinetry exaggerated the feeling of gloom. RIGHT: Warming drawers are placed next to the wall ovens to keep, dishes hot between helpings.

pietra. Comparable in price to granite, pietra is more forgiving of stains and scratches. To prevent countertops from being obscured by shadows, the owner asked for a combination of recessed, hanging, and undercounter fixtures to target every task. "You want the light in front of you and over your work surface, not behind your head," she says.

"We're seeing a swing away from the all-inclusive great-room kitchen," Steve adds. "Many people prefer a kitchen-as-workshop model, particularly when it's unified visually and architecturally with the breakfast or dining space, as this one turned out to be."

Vintage Country

Expanding from 80 to 286 s.f. while retaining a period appeal

Whard Megan and Nicholas Dixon bought a turn-of-the-century cottage in Northern California wine country, they never imagined how it would change their lives. At the time, 1987, both worked in San Francisco—she as a graphic designer and he as an engineer—and they only got to go up there on weekends. But they fell so hopelessly in love with the location that when Megan discovered she was pregnant with the second of their two children, the couple sold their home in the city and moved to their wine-country retreat.

The good news was that within a year, Nicholas was able to quit commuting when he found a job only 30 minutes away. The bad news was that the house's shortcomings became major hassles when they had to live with them every day. The kitchen, for instance, though serviceable, was far too cramped. The couple made do for two years, then called in architect James McCalligan, from nearby Santa Rosa, to reconfigure the 1,800-square-foot dwelling, with the cooking area as the top priority. "The Dixons approached their house exactly the right way," says Steve Thomas. "If you can stand to live with your new place long enough to learn its strengths and weaknesses, you're in a better position to engage in the renovation process with your architect or kitchen designer."

ABOVE: Although charming, the original kitchen was cramped and inefficient. RIGHT: With its beadboard walls and 1950s range, the airy new space takes its cue from old-fashioned farmhouses. It isn't locked in the past, though; the range hood, refrigerator and microwave are all contemporary.

PROBLEM

"This was never meant to be a fancy house," says Megan. Over the years, the place had been added onto in a way that "made no sense," says McCalligan. A small, 7-by-8-foot mudroom and a narrow water-heater closet that included a toilet were tacked onto the back of the kitchen. A shelf-lined extension of the living room doubled as a passageway between that space and the kitchen and as a pantry housing the refrigerator. The kitchen itself had no dishwasher and no storage space other than one L-shaped bank of cabinetry. "There was really nothing worth saving," says Megan.

SOLUTION

One feature that affected the design and orientation of the new kitchen was the addition of a flagstone paved courtyard at the back of the house. This gave the room a focus by allowing the architect to open it up to the backyard via glass doors. "The courtyard really expands the outdoor living possibilities," says Steve. "It's ideally located for grilling, cocktails, and dining." To expand the kitchen itself—from just over 80 square feet to 286 square feet—McCalligan claimed part of a bedroom, plus the mudroom and a closet; he also turned the old passage/pantry space into a hallway to a great room beyond.

To inspire their architect, the Dixons chose a restored enamel cookstove dating from the 1950s, which McCalligan made the showpiece of the kitchen. To meet building codes, he installed a new hood over it, choosing one that wouldn't detract from the gleaming appliance beneath. "When

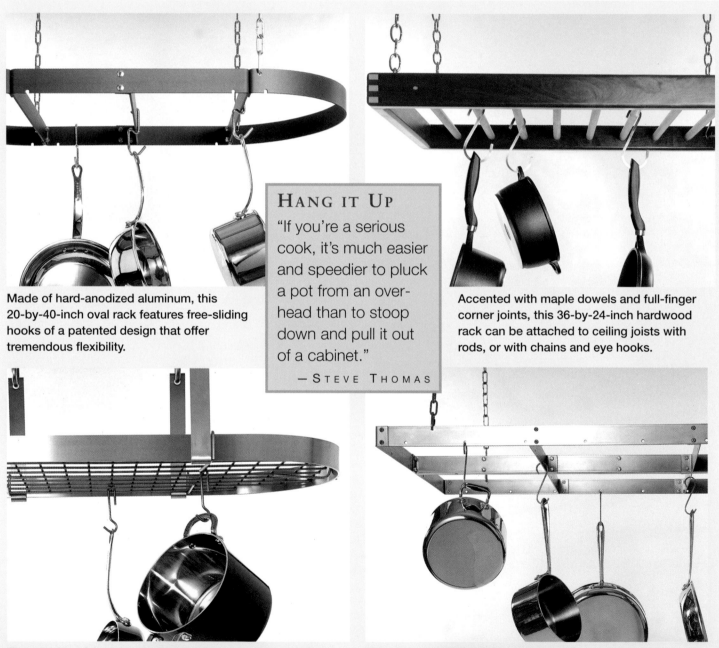

Made of hard-anodized aluminum, this 20-by-40-inch oval rack features free-sliding hooks of a patented design that offer tremendous flexibility.

HANG IT UP

"If you're a serious cook, it's much easier and speedier to pluck a pot from an overhead than to stoop down and pull it out of a cabinet."

— STEVE THOMAS

Accented with maple dowels and full-finger corner joints, this 36-by-24-inch hardwood rack can be attached to ceiling joists with rods, or with chains and eye hooks.

The 41½-by-18-inch brushed-stainless rack with mounting straps has a dual-purpose gridded center: Lids can be stored on top of it, and pots can be hung anywhere from the grid.

This stainless-steel chef's rack has a faux pewter finish. It measures 48 by 28 inches and comes with 32 pot hooks, each 4½ inches long.

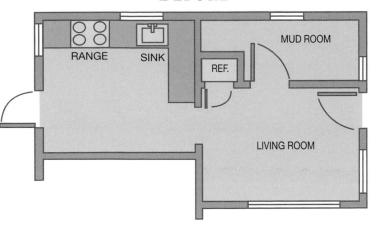

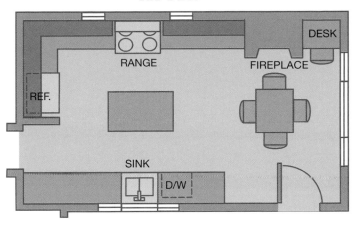

design is done right, it's like a good haircut," says Steve. "You shouldn't notice it."

McCalligan, who had the cabinets built locally, designed them to appear as old-fashioned as possible. To add natural light, he installed windows behind the wall cabinets that flank the range hood. In lieu of an island, the Dixons opted for an antique farm table. The pot rack, made of old wood, was chosen for a similar reason. A new maple-strip floor matches others in the house.

FINISHING TOUCHES

A pale color palette and a stainless-steel–faced refrigerator tucked into its own alcove keep the space from looking like it emerged from a time capsule. The walls in the cooking area received a

LEFT: Small windows behind two cabinets allow light to filter through a collection of vintage glassware.
ABOVE: Tweaking the floor plan created a windowed dining area.

soft sage-green paint; the eating area is butter yellow and warmed by a gas-powered fireplace. "That was my big indulgence," Megan says (the original plan had simply called for a bench). "It makes the kitchen an even cozier place to eat," she says. Now that their home is truly livable, the family has no regrets about their move. "We'd never go back to the city," Megan says. ∎

Equippin

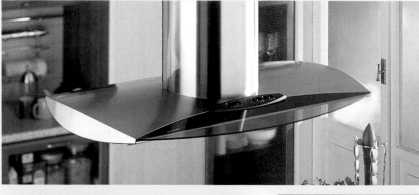

g Your Kitchen

CHOOSING THE COMPONENTS OF YOUR WORKSPACE

ENTER A KITCHEN SHOW ROOM OR THE AISLES OF A HOME center, and the variety of kitchen fixtures and appliances will boggle your mind. It's easy to think that you need all this gear. Not true. Although your kitchen is probably the hub of your household, it doesn't have to do everything. Serious cooks often describe their ideal kitchen as a workshop, and that philosophy can keep you focused on what you need. The best workshops, after all, contain only what's necessary to get the job done. So wrestle your old floor plan into a model of thoughtful workflow, but choose the equipment carefully. This chapter describes some of the choices, including a few you might not think of. Just remember who you're cooking for and why you're cooking. If you do, your equipment will reflect your way of working, just as a kitchen should.

Anatomy of a Kitchen Cabinet

In search of a well-made kitchen cabinet

KITCHEN SHOWROOMS ARE EMPORIUMS OF GRAND illusion. The floors always glisten, countertops are uncluttered by coffemakers, and the cabinets, well, the cabinets are always perfect: no scratches, no dings, none of your 3-year-old's favorite stickers, no dishes crammed into too-small shelves. These same cabinets are stained in the latest colors, floated under 16-foot ceilings (so you'll never notice how tall they're not), and lit by several thousand watts of halogen firepower. When the doors swing shut with resounding thumps and the drawers slide to a firm stop, you're sold. Too bad. You think you bought furniture that will last a lifetime, but you probably got dressed-up orange crates that will last barely a decade. Top-quality kitchen cabinets are made like good furniture, but even the most devoted watchers of the Food Network don't know what to look for. Worse, what you should be looking for is usually hidden. So what follows is a guide to the guts of a cabinet. The one shown here is a finely crafted—but unassembled—base cabinet made by a family-owned company that has only one line of cabinetry: the good stuff. Get to know its features, and look for them on your next cabinet.

ASSEMBLED

THE WELL-BUILT CABINET FACE. All pieces visible from the front of a cabinet are its face. The wood used on the face of a quality cabinet shouldn't have knots, pitch pockets, sanding scars, grain irregularities or color differences. **1.** Face-frame stiles and rails are joined with long tenons (protruding wood tongues) and deep mortises (the slots into which tenons fit). Where two pieces of wood meet in a joint, the line between them almost disappears. **2.** Drawer fronts are cut from a single piece of solid wood. **3.** Flat door panels are made from solid pieces of wood. **END PANEL.** This is the side of a cabinet exposed to view. **4.** Solid wood is chosen for similarity of grain and color. **5.** Frame pieces have mortise-and-tenon joinery; the assembled panel is attached to the carcass (a plywood box) with screws driven from the inside out. **DRAWER.** All sides are made from hardwood ⅝ inch or thicker. **6.** All sides are routed with a groove that supports the drawer base. **7.** Joints are dovetailed at all corners. **CARCASS.** This plywood box forms the cabinet interior, seen here lying on a side panel. **8.** Side and floor panels are at least ½ inch thick. **9.** Plywood shelves are at least ¾ inch thick. **10.** The cabinet's floor and back fit into routed side panels.

FACE

END PANEL

UNASSEMBLED

DRAWER

CARCASS

DETAILS THAT MAKE A DIFFERENCE

1. TUNEABLE HINGES Whether visible or hidden, a hinge should be not only strong but also adjustable so that doors can be aligned as needed with the surrounding face-frame.

2. FLOATING PANELS The frames around panels on the cabinet doors and on the exposed side of the cabinet have deep grooves. Panels aren't glued or fastened into the grooves, which allows them to expand and contract with changes in temperature and humidity without cracking or pushing the frame apart. Tiny pads keep the panels centered.

3. DRAWER SLIDES A drawer supported by two side-mounted slides is much stronger than one that runs over a single slide centered underneath. The quietest slides run on nylon bearings. A good, full-extension slide can carry loads of at least 75 pounds and will allow a drawer to open fully.

4. FRAME-TO-CARCASS JOINTS A strong connection between the carcass and the face frame (the five narrow pieces of wood that surround the drawer and the doors) is a mark of quality craftsmanship. At the bottom corner of the back of the face frame, the vertical piece (stile) has a wide groove, which locks onto the side panel of the carcass. The narrow groove across the horizontal piece (rail) lines up with an identical groove in the floor of the cabinet. Biscuits glued into these grooves join the rail to the cabinet floor.

5. SHELF LOCKS Shelves should be adjustable and supported by metal brackets, not plastic ones. To keep the shelf from wandering, a locking device such as a plastic retainer plugs into an adjustment hole above.

1

4

CABINETS & STORAGE

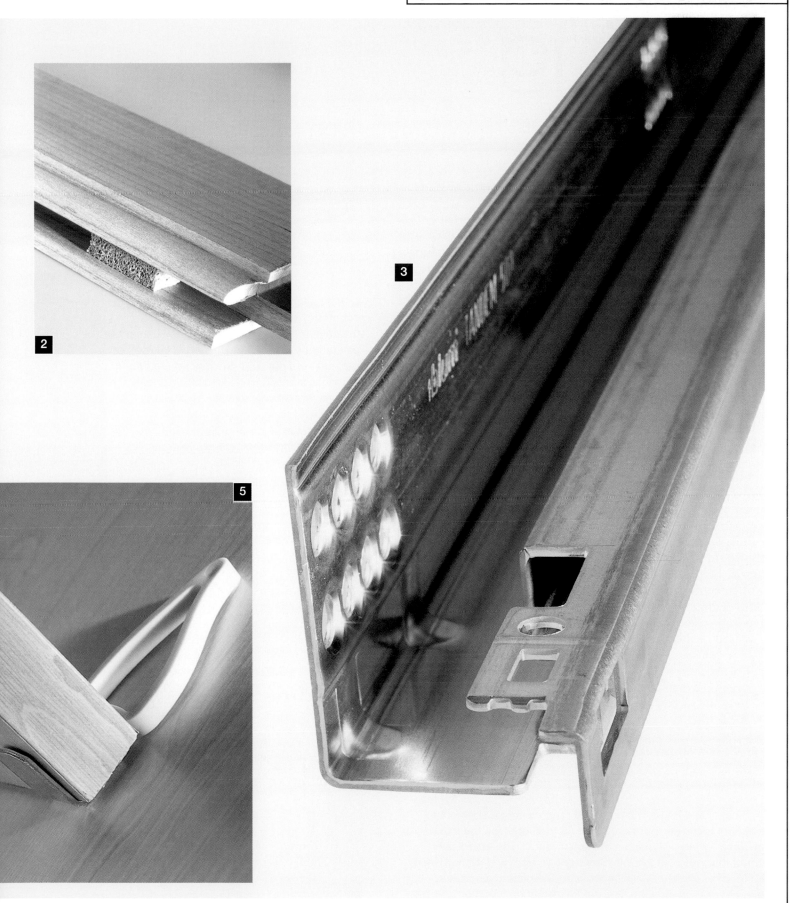

95

Facing Facts

All it takes to give some old cabinets a new look is a thin skin of wood

AFTER LIVING IN THE SAME HOUSE FOR NEARLY 25 years, Jim and Susan Sidel were finally ready to part ways—with their old kitchen. They conjured up a vision of what the room could be, with new cabinets and countertops, tile backsplashes, and stainless-steel appliances. Then a contractor handed them an estimate of more than $40,000 and said the project would take three to four months to complete. Disheartened, the Sidels began looking for other options and found a cabinet-refacing company near their home. They were impressed with the quality of the company's past projects, and taking their bid would cut the overall cost of their new kitchen by half. "When we learned it would only take a week, we were sold," says Jim. Another remodeling project (see photos) didn't even disturb existing countertops.

Refacing works on the principle that beauty is only skin deep, and a new skin of wood or plastic just 1/40 of an inch thick is all it takes to turn an ugly-duckling kitchen into a swan. Rather than go through the messy process of tearing out structurally sound cabinets, refacing contractors remove only the old doors and drawer fronts, swapping them with factory-prefinished replacements. They leave the existing face frames and end panels in place and cover them with a matching wood or plastic veneer. New drawer slides and hardware complete the transformation, which typically costs between $4,000 and $8,000.

A top-quality veneering job begins with good surface preparation. Loose stiles and rails should be secured and the finish either deglazed or removed entirely. This ensures a solid bond between the old surface and the veneer. Cracks and imperfections in the surface are filled with putty and sanded smooth.

Some installers use veneers with a pressure-sensitive adhesive backing, but others think contact cement applied on-site provides a superior, more moisture-resistant bond.

Lisa and Jonathan Giles had a new tile countertop in their kitchen, so replacing the cabinets didn't make sense. They tried painting the dark woodwork white (ABOVE), but the finish cracked. So they refaced the frames with maple veneer to brighten the kitchen. Not all cabinets are good candidates for refacing, however—refacing glues won't work on particleboard. Solid-wood face frames, however, can almost always be refaced.

For the Giles refacing job, the contractor sanded down the face frames (1) to degloss the paint. He applied contact cement to both the frames and veneer strips (2) then pressed the thin wood in place. Where two pieces of veneer met in a seam, he overlaped them and cut the joint line through both with a sharp utility knife. After peeling away the excess (3) he found a perfectly mated seam. In refacing, this kind of attention to detail pays off.

2

3

Glass Acts

This sleek, infinitely cleanable material can enhance cabinets in surprising ways

WHEN HELEN COLLEY, CO-OWNER of *This Old House*'s project house in Key West, Florida, first laid eyes on an etched glass-front drawer in a catalog, she knew she'd found the inspiration for the kitchen her husband, Michael Miller, was designing. Never mind that a glass drawer seemed somewhat impractical: If a heavy object were to fall on an open drawer, the glass—although tempered—might break. But she couldn't resist. "Glass," she says, "is an interesting and beautiful complement to the cherry and granite that are also prominent in the room."

Colley's choice reflects the increasing popularity of glass as a kitchen accent material, suitable for not only drawers but also cabinet doors, backsplashes, drawer pulls, range hoods, and cooktops. "Glass-front cabinets are a traditional part of Greek Revival architecture," says *This Old House* host Steve Thomas. "But the current trend owes as much to a growing interest in luxury items for the kitchen as to the streamlined, elegant effect of glass."

ABOVE: Steve Thomas pops in the glass front of a drawer in the kitchen of the Key West house. RIGHT: Corn-colored glass tiles form a luminescent backsplash.

In a variety of colors and textures, glass tiles add drama to any kitchen backsplash—and they're low maintenance.

LIGHT AND AIR

Typically as inconspicuous as a '57 Chevy in a swimming pool, range hoods have rarely served as attractive focal points for kitchens. But by combining glass with stainless steel, kitchen designers are transforming these utilitarian vents into high-tech sculpture. This chimney-style hood, designed in Italy and illuminated by four 12-volt halogen lamps, has a curved glass shield and hangs above an island range. Although the hood measures 42 inches across—enough to contain the smoke and fumes from a 36-inch-long cooktop—its transparency makes it look delicate and practically inconspicuous.

MAKING GLASS LAST

Except for sandblasted surfaces, which need a penetrating silicone-based finish to seal out grime, glass is virtually stainproof. A spritz of glass cleaner is usually enough to maintain the luster of kitchen tiles, knobs, and cabinet parts made of the material. Range hoods, cooktops, and other surfaces where grease tends to gather may require more muscle power but should be scrubbed with only a sponge or soft rag, along with a degreasing dish detergent. Although durable, glass will chip or crack if used inappropriately. To be safe, think about your kitchen's traffic pattern and take a tip from Helen Colley, who situated the glass drawers in her kitchen far from the dishwasher—where loading a slippery pot could be hazardous—and intends to fill them with washcloths and towels. A liner could open other possibilities.

GLASS GRABS

Pressed-glass knobs designed to look like cut glass are an inexpensive way to add a dash of color and a glint of light to a kitchen. "They're really popular and have an appeal that harkens back to the Victorian era," says Kellie Krug, of Restoration Hardware, which sells the knobs shown above. Glass drawer-pulls have long been popular in bathrooms, but in their new, deep-jewel-tone colors they're also appropriate accents in both contemporary and country kitchens. Says Alice Hayes, of Kitchens by Deane in Stamford, Connecticut, "Glass adds a certain sparkle that nickel, chrome, or brass just can't match."

Open Shelving

Storage without doors can make a stuffy kitchen downright homey

THE 1887 QUEEN ANNE IN A HISTORIC NEIGHBORHOOD was an unlikely candidate for major rehabilitation: There was nothing terribly wrong with it. Nevertheless, new owners decided they could make it better. Their mission: to build a 21st-century infrastructure into the 19th-century house while maintaining its character. On the aesthetic side, they wanted to maximize the natural light. And, although the kitchen was workable, "it was someone's idea of a dream kitchen 30 years ago," one of the owners recalls.

From the start, the couple knew the level of finish they desired throughout their home: All new walls would be plaster (no drywall), and all woodwork would be restored—or replaced—to match the original. In other words, the house would continue to look as if it hadn't been touched since it was built.

The Shaker-style wood cabinets in the kitchen have simple brown button pulls. "We painted the cabinets different colors—a cream and a pale pea soup—to blur the line between cabinetry and furniture," says architect Charles Myer. But at one end of the kitchen, Myer wanted to set off a breakfast corner and create, as he says, "a visual conclusion to the room." This he did in two ways: one, by designing a built-in L-shaped banquette (with drawers at one end for phone books and miscellany); and two, by lining the wall around it with a series of shelves supported by wood brackets (facing page). Millworkers built the shelves from Myer's design. The ¾-inch-thick, 10-inch-deep shelves and the ½-inch-thick brackets and ledger strips behind them are made from poplar. To accommodate a window in the corner, Myer curved the ends of the shelves—those on the long wall are convex; those that abut the window trim on the adjoining wall are concave. Shelves are installed 23⅓ inches apart and are grooved to support plates. Another 6-inch-deep shelf runs above both sets, and it is outlined in deep burgundy paint.

Open shelves, no matter what the color scheme, do a lot to knock some of the formal stuffing out of a new kitchen. The kitchens here will show you what's possible.

TOP: Fir shelves, 9¼-inch-deep and a generous 14 inches apart, are 20 inches from the countertop and supported by strong wrought-iron brackets. BOTTOM: Deep red-sienna paint highlights the white dishes and marble counters in this pantry. FACING: A new banquette was surrounded with new, old-looking shelves.

The Ultimate Sink

Take time to pick the right sink—you'll spend a lot of time in front of it

NOT MANY YEARS AGO, REDOING A KITCHEN meant tough decisions about everything except the kitchen sink. The sink was simple: white-enameled cast iron or silvery stainless steel; one bowl or two. Now, picking a sink requires more research than selecting a computer.

There are farm sinks, pantry sinks, vegetable sinks, and half sinks. Sinks for corners, islands, bars, and counters. Most of them are round or square, but some are shaped like amoebas. They are gold-plated, solid brass, slate, stone, fireclay, and plastic. They are $29 and tinny or $2,300 and solid copper. Some would look just fine flanked by Renoirs.

Jim and Kristen Galefs's search for the ideal sink is nothing less than an odyssey. And they need two. They think it will be simple. It isn't. Yet all they want are friendly, old-fashioned sinks that will hold up well for a family of six in the new kitchen addition to their 75-year-old house in Greenwich, Connecticut.

Diligent consumers, they arrive early one morning at a swank kitchen-and-bath store in nearby Stamford. They seem a bit bleary-eyed from a night of browsing the Internet ("Did you know you can buy a sink online?" Jim asks.) They are guided in their search by designer Terry Scarborough and Steve Thomas, whose interest in kitchens ranges from designing them to cooking in them. "Especially anything Thai," he says.

First stop: a display featuring a cast-iron farm sink. The front, or apron, of the sink is exposed so it looks like a washtub set above the cabinetry. The basin is big. Steve, wielding his tape measure, calls out (continued on p. 106)

Homeowners Jim and Kristen Galef, left, with kitchen designer Terry Scarborough and *This Old House* host Steve Thomas. Their mission: selecting a pair of sinks for the kitchen addition to the Galef's 75-year-old Connecticut home.

ONE BASIN OR TWO?

1. **Composite** one and a half bowls ($460). Resembles enameled cast iron but weighs less. Color-through material means chips and scratches shouldn't show. Lighter colors are more likely to show staining and scorching.

2. **Hammered-brass** single bowl ($565). Flashy, opulent, and expensive, brass is durable but best reserved for sinks that are seldom used. It dents easily and requires polishing to maintain its luster.

3. **Stainless-steel** double bowl ($765). High-quality models stand up under heavy use and are highly resistant to stains and heat. Choosing 20 gauge or heavier 18 gauge helps prevent dents. Look for an insulating coating on the underside to dampen noise.

4. **Americast** double bowl ($375). Porcelain enameled over a proprietary metal and composite base. Americast looks like cast iron, but it's lighter and less costly.

5. **Fireclay** square and disposal bowl ($290 and $204). The finish is as durable as porcelain enamel, but the sink could crack and chip if something heavy is dropped in it.

6. **Fireclay** single bowl ($1,358). Looks like cast iron but is significantly lighter and normally less expensive. Unlike cast iron, it can be intricately detailed, as in the design on the apron of this pantry sink.

7. **Solid-surface** double bowl with drainboard ($430). Stains, gouges and scratches are easily repaired by scrubbing with a nylon pad. But it's not as resistant to heat as other materials and may scorch.

8. **Solid-surface** double bowl ($525). A "seamless" joint is possible between solid-surface countertop and sink, leaving no place for dirt to lodge.

9. **Soapstone** single bowl with backsplash ($800 to $1,200). Made from stone slabs ¾ to 1¼ inches thick. Holds heat well and is easy to maintain—can be cleaned with just about anything. Heavy (this one weighs 300 pounds) and generally custom-made.

10. **Vikrell** double bowl ($300). Fiberglass makes this composite more resistant to heat and stains than other composites. Available in matte or gloss finish.

1

5

6

7

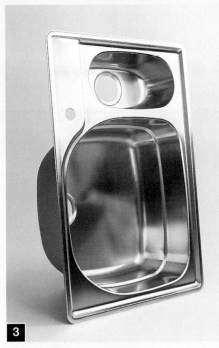

3

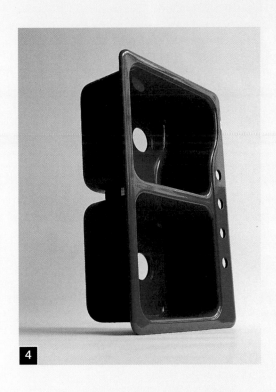

4

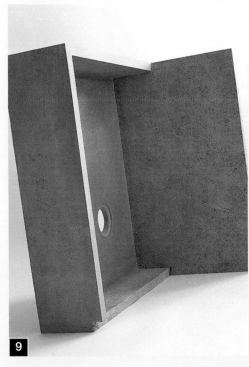

9

10

the dimensions like numbers in a bingo game: "Length 33, width 22, depth 8."

Kristen's nose wrinkles slightly. "It's nice, but it says 'country.' My kitchen is more formal—English manorish—with mahogany cabinets and granite countertops. The interior decorator wants us to put in a copper sink."

"Is the decorator going to clean it for you?" Steve asks. Copper looks great until the first time someone runs water in it. Then it requires polishing and a gentle hand to be sure it does not get dinged. Not right for the Galefs, who have three children and a fourth on the way.

Next up is a composite sink, made of quartz or granite particles suspended in plastic. Jim knocks on the sides of the basin, producing a hollow thud. "It reminds me of those plastic bathtubs." Strike composite from the list. Also, based on the Galefs' past research, rule out solid surfacing such as Corian (not "right" for granite counters), stone (too expensive) and brass (too hard to clean).

At this point, Terry's carefully drawn kitchen plans are unfurled across the showroom countertop and debate over the configuration of the sinks begins. There's a prep sink on the island and a second sink used for cleanup under east-facing windows and next to the dishwasher.

"Nice layout," Steve says, leaning over the plans. The cleanup sink has two bowls, one wide and deep for pots and pans and a second shallower one for delicate items. Bar sinks (averaging 15 by 15 inches) are typically used as prep sinks, but Steve believes they are too small. The Galefs resolve to pick a larger-than-average prep sink and the biggest double-bowl sink they can find. They can't decide which sink is more deserving of the garbage disposer, so they opt to install one in each.

Most sinks come with three to five predrilled holes in the deck, or back, for the faucets, sprayer and various types of dispensers. The Galefs will include a soap dispenser (beats a big plastic bottle next to the sink) and a hot water dispenser at the prep sink.

The first round of decisions made, the group heads off to a kitchen sink supermarket in nearby Norwalk. Hundreds of examples in every size, shape and color hang in rows from

Given the importance of a sink in any kitchen, choosing one is a team effort. A kitchen designer has access to sinks you couldn't get otherwise.

the walls. It's here that Steve launches his bid for stainless. It complements commecial appliances, holds up well, and is affordable and easy to clean. Some models have a coating on the underside that deadens the rattle of dishes. The coating also insulates the sink to keep dishwater hot.

"But doesn't stainless scratch?" Kristen asks. A brushed finish helps disguise scratches, Terry says, and a sink with a high nickel-chromium content is resistant to rust, pitting and stains. But no matter what materials you choose, a sink will scratch, stain, chip, or dent. "There's no such thing as an indestructible sink," she concludes.

"I guess I'm picturing a big, white cast-iron sink," Kirsten sighs. "It's what my mother always had. It's what I grew up with."

Along the walls are a dozen or so cast-iron sinks. Steve pulls out his tape measure once again to determine which is biggest. "Cast iron is great," he says. "I like its sturdiness and durability. Treated right—no abrasive cleaners—the finish will hold up."

A self-rimming model that measures 38 by 22 inches with one 10-inch-deep bowl and a smaller 7-inch-deep bowl has plenty of room for all the dishes generated by a family of six. In white, it's just right.

That settled, the Galefs turn their attention to the prep sink. Nearby is a 16-by-20-inch fireclay sink. Similar to vitreous china (the stuff toilets are made of), fireclay resembles cast iron but has a softer sheen. It's also lightweight and fragile—a problem when using it as a cleanup sink but acceptable in a prep sink. This becomes sink number two.

Terry, Steve, Jim and Kirsten give a collective sigh of relief. After five hours of legwork and additional time spent doing research, asking the advice of friends and experts and, of course, checking out the Internet, the Galefs have their sinks. "Well," says Steve, "now you can move on to appliances, flooring, lighting, wall coverings . . . anything else?"

TOP: Pale yellow has always been a cheery alternative to beige. Rather than blanketing a whole kitchen in a lemon hue, try using it as an accent in sinks. CENTER: This island sink supplements the main sink (in background), providing an additional station when you entertain. BOTTOM: This sink is just big enough for modest food prep and making drinks.

Splendid Spigots

Remember when a faucet was just a faucet?

NOT MANY YEARS AGO, THE FAUCET WAS THE PLAIN Jane of the American kitchen and bathroom, a utilitarian pair of valves that magically filled basins with the mere flick of a wrist. Turn the lever one way: running water. But inside and out, faucets have evolved from the simple to the sublime. The mechanics of the modern faucet can be enough to perplex even a devoted handyman. With ceramic discs, washerless cartridges, rotating ball valves, and more plastic parts than a new car, there's a lot to know about buying or fixing a faucet.

Such inner complexity is reflected in exterior design as well: More than 500 different versions of the device are now available. "In the 1950s, everything was ceramic white or chrome," says *This Old House* plumber Richard Trethewey. "Now faucets have become something of a fashion statement." Expensive

Brass needs a tarnish-stopping finish, so Chicago Faucet's José Sandoval gives racks of buffed spouts a dip in electrified vats of curry-colored chrome solution.

metals and high-tech plastics are turning faucets into complex expressions of design. Some levers look like intricate medical devices; others are sculpted into forms that seem worthy of art gallery display. Spouts have become small fountains or long-necked, trumpetless swans. Flexible pipe is as common as solid. Metals wear coats of paint, Teflon, pewter, copper, plastic, brass, gold, nickel, or silver.

Modern faucets are designed to "please the eye and gratify the soul," according to one faucet manufacturer. Where once water ran straight and uninspired, now it's a deluge, a cascade, a waterfall of possibilities. But once you know just what makes a faucet work (sidebar, right), you'll make a more informed choice.

LEFT: There's room for even the biggest kitchen pot under the 13-inch-high spout of this faucet. It replicates an old French design, one of the first to mix hot and cold water in a single spout. BELOW: This old-fashioned barber faucet has a spout-mounted sprayer.

THE HEART OF A FAUCET

Faucet valves are easy to take for granted, until they start leaking. Then the telltale drip, drip, drip makes their insides the subject of annoyed fascination.

There are four basic valve types: compression, ball, cartridge, and disc. The old-fashioned compression valve works the same way the Little Dutch Boy's finger plugged a leaking dike: A soft material (a washer) is pressed firmly against a harder one (the valve seat) to keep water from seeping out. Constant wear and hard-water deposits eat away both washers and seats; fortunately, new ones are easily installed.

A ball valve, which controls temperature and flow with a single lever, has a perforated brass or plastic sphere that moves like a hip joint. The ball and it's spring-loaded washers are susceptible to wear and may need frequent replacement.

Super-smooth white ceramic discs, made of aluminum oxide, promise long, leak-free service; old-style washers are cheaper and considerably easier to replace.

A cartridge valve encases a pierced stainless cylinder in pierced plastic. Turning the handle (or lever) lines up the holes so the water flows. When it leaks, the entire one-piece assembly must be replaced.

Disc valves have a mated pair of perforated wafers so smooth no water can pass until the discs' holes align. Ceramic discs have conquered Europe, and Richard Trethewey predicts they'll be in most U.S. faucets soon. Beware of low-end valves with plastic discs—they wear quickly. What's more, fixing ceramic is expensive. A new ceramic disc valve can run at least $12, while a washer for a compression valve costs about 30 cents.

From the outside, both valves look the same, but the one on the left turns a ceramic disc, while the one on the right compresses a rubber washer against a metal seat.

Muscle Stoves

Power meets precision in a stainless-steel cooking machine

SNOW PEAS HISS. LAMB CHOPS SIZZLE. FLAMES LEAP and steam billows as two cooks jostle against a backdrop of grease-spattered stainless steel and blazing gas burners. The heat, the commotion, and, above all, the hulking, bulletproof stove at the center of all this suggest a busy night at Lespinasse, L'Orangerie, or some other four-star eatery. But beyond the bustle of cooking, there's no minimalist dining room, impenetrable menu, unctuous waiters, or haughty sommelier. And we've seen one of those cooks before: It's Steve Thomas, scullery guy.

This is no restaurant galley, but the confusion is understandable. Steve and cookbook author Nina Simonds are vigorously stir-frying, boiling, grilling, and baking in the showroom of Clarke Distribution, a high-end appliance wholesaler in Hopkinton, Massachusetts. And the range they're toiling over could easily pass for a professional chef's beloved behemoth. At 48 inches wide and a whopping 615 pounds, "This is the four-wheel-drive truck of stoves," says Steve, flipping a grilled-to-perfection salmon steak. "If you can't get where you want to go driving one of these babies, forget it—you just can't get there."

Kitchen designers from New England and beyond send their clients to Clarke to pant, drool, and even do a little cooking on these massive, powerful-looking appliances. But Steve and Nina know that one nicely grilled fish does not a quality stove make, so they're also whipping up her recipes for poached pears, pancakes, whole wheat bread, cashew chicken, and chocolate chip cookies as they test-drive the newest generation of professional-style stoves. While no one doubts that they pack serious heat, our team seeks to explore their subtleties to learn if these cookers can really simmer as well as they sear, and whether they broil effectively, bake evenly, and (don't forget) clean up easily.

To perfect them for consumer kitchens, stove manufacturers have been tweaking their wares for nearly two decades. Jim Raftus, Clarke's marketing director, says the demand for these stoves really took off in the early eighties, when chefs longed for the same blowtorch-burner power at home that they enjoyed on the job. "They'd put Vulcans or Blodgetts into their kitchens and pack in insulation themselves so they could do a zero-clearance installation," he says. "After them came

Minutes away from a wonderful feast, Steve Thomas lifts ginger-teriyaki salmon steaks from the big stove's grill and onto a platter held by cookbook author Nina Simonds. "A basic advantage of these stoves is simply that they're bigger," says Steve. "Two people can easily cook on one at the same time."

people who love to cook, or who love to look like they love to cook. The manufacturers noticed this was more than a passing fad and started adapting their stoves for the home market."

Today, nearly a dozen companies make pro-style ranges and cooktops (ranges without ovens), and prosperous boomers with sophisticated palates willingly fork over the $3,000 to $9,000 required to join the club. Toss in installation and the requisite—and equally powerful—vent hood (see page 114), and the tally can top $12,000.

Steve inspects a 48-inch-wide, 6-burner range. The oven door he's holding is so stout that he could stand on it without causing even the slightest bend.

"When you're shelling out that kind of money," says Steve, "you need to do some homework."

Superficially, all muscle stoves seem the same. They feature potent gas burners, which generally peak at 15,000 Btu versus the 10,000-Btu flame on a standard stove. While the color palette has broadened to (continued on p. 114)

The King Of Cookers

Commercial-style stoves offer cooking versatility as well as flame power. They're available in 30-, 36-, 48-, and 60-inch widths, and manufacturers offer virtually any conceivable combination of burners, grills, griddles, and ovens.

"This is the four-wheel-drive truck of stoves. If you can't get where you want to go driving one of these babies, forget it—you just can't get there" —**Steve Thomas**

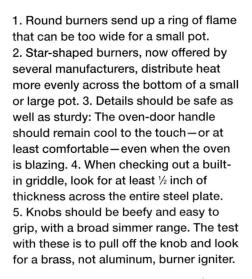

1. Round burners send up a ring of flame that can be too wide for a small pot. 2. Star-shaped burners, now offered by several manufacturers, distribute heat more evenly across the bottom of a small or large pot. 3. Details should be safe as well as sturdy: The oven-door handle should remain cool to the touch—or at least comfortable—even when the oven is blazing. 4. When checking out a built-in griddle, look for at least ½ inch of thickness across the entire steel plate. 5. Knobs should be beefy and easy to grip, with a broad simmer range. The test with these is to pull off the knob and look for a brass, not aluminum, burner igniter.

include black, deep green, and even white; polished stainless steel is far and away the most common choice. Most brands can be purchased with a wide array of options such as a built-in lava-rock grill or a cast-iron griddle; one manufacturer even offers a 30,000-Btu wok burner that resembles a Saturn V thruster. "It doesn't sell in New England, but in California, it's huge," says Jill Fotiades, Clarke's showroom guide.

Peering beneath the shiny skins of a showroom's worth of stoves reveals that, for all their similarities, they have some important differences. Burners, for example, can be sealed or open. Many homeowners prefer the sealed version: Any boil-overs or spills drip no farther than the burner well, where they're easily wiped away. Open burners permit erupting bouillabaisse to trickle down to removable drip trays, sometimes splashing onto other parts of the stove's innards. But many professional chefs opt for the open style because air rushing up through the gap between the burner and the well allows the flames to lick higher and hotter.

Simmering was once a weakness of these stoves, because their blast-furnace burners could not be cranked low enough. Today, electronics automatically cycle the flame on and off. At the lowest setting, for example, a burner runs for just 10 seconds a minute, effectively lowering the output to a caressing 375 Btu compared with the 1,000-Btu minimum for a standard gas stove.

Besides the sealed-unsealed options, burners also come in two different shapes. Round burners throw a ring of flame, which can be a problem with a small pot if the fire encircles it rather than heating the bottom. "With these you might have to replace some of your cookware with larger restaurant-size pans," says Steve. The other type, a star-shaped burner, spreads heat more evenly.

In earlier versions of these stoves, ovens that heated slowly could frustrate a harried cook. "Most serious cooks prefer gas for the stovetop, but a gas oven can take a half-hour to get going," says Tom Clarke, president of his eponymous company. "That's not a problem in a commercial kitchen, where the oven is on all day. But nobody wants to come home and wait 30 minutes just to start heating up chicken fingers for the kids." Manufacturers have responded with a new generation of "dual fuel" ranges that have gas burners up top but electric ovens underneath. "The oven heats up in 10 minutes," says Clarke. "Nobody goes hungry."

BIG-STOVE HOOD

With nearly double the heat output of standard stoves, commercial-style cookers need powerful hoods. The Home Ventilating Institute, a testing agency, recommends a minimum air flow of 100 cubic feet per minute (cfm) for a standard 30-inch cooktop. But the hoods that go with these stoves move air much faster: from 600 to 1,400 cfm, depending on the width. A powerful blower, however, can produce irritating noise. The solution: Place the blower outside the house or in the duct between the hood and the exhaust vent.

Like the stoves they serve, most of these hoods, which cost $1,500 to $2,500, have stainless-steel enclosures. Features to look for include a variable-speed blower control, a thermostatic control switch that automatically turns the blower on when the air over the stove heats up, halogen lights, and aluminum baffle filters, the type used in restaurant hoods, which have greater surface area for capturing grease and smoke particles.

After a hood is up and running, it must be used properly to prevent grease buildup and contain odors. Instead of waiting until you see the steam or smell the onions to turn it on, get in the habit of clearing the air as soon as you fire up the stove.

The 60-inch hood in this Lexington, Massachusetts, kitchen (TOP), has an outside-mounted blower which minimizes noise. ABOVE LEFT: Richard Silva holds the hood canopy while Charlie Silva fastens it. ABOVE RIGHT: Charlie mounts the blower housing over the 10-inch exhaust opening.

Clearing the Air

Proper venting—up or down—keeps grease and steam out of the kitchen

family of four produces
nough steam in a year's
ooking to equal 12 gallons
f water. Vent hoods redirect
hat moisture—and the
ccompanying grease.

THE SHRIMP STIR-FRY WAS A HIT WITH YOUR dinner guests, but your wallpaper won't be thanking you. Last week's pasta in garlic sauce? You don't even want to know what it's doing to your cabinets. "An average family produces over a gallon of airborne grease in their cooking every year," says Karen Collins, a manager at Broan-NuTone, the nation's biggest maker of vent hoods. "Now, where do you think that stuff is going?"

Without some sort of ventilation system to whisk it away, all the by-products of cooking—grease, heat, steam, odors, and smoke—will settle on whatever surfaces they find, turning appliances sticky, eating away at cabinet finishes, and yellowing ceilings and wallcoverings. Unfortunately, most building codes around the country don't require kitchen ventilation. And homeowners, if they've given it any thought at all, have been turned off by experiences with noisy, ineffective, and hard-to-clean hoods. Responding to these complaints, the makers of kitchen vents now produce units that are more efficient, quiet, and easy to clean, as well as more stylish.

Venting systems come in two varieties: recirculating or ducted. Recirculating hoods suck the air up from the cooktop, push it through a mesh screen and charcoal filter to trap grease and odors, then blow it back into the room. Ducted systems draw the air through a filter or grease collector, then push it outdoors. According to *This Old House* contractor Tom Silva, ducted systems are superior. "I've never found the recirculating ones to really work," he says. Even the makers of these systems admit to their limitations. "If you can't put in a duct, a ductless is better than nothing," says Collins. "But it's better to get the pollutants out."

There are two basic ways to get bad air out: with hoods, which are mounted over a range or cooktop to draw air up and out, and with downdraft systems, which pull smoke and grease down and out through a vent located at cooktop level. For both types, the ducts can run through walls or ceilings or even under the floor. "The shorter the run and the fewer elbows, the better," says Tom. That's why the ideal setup is a hood mounted right against, and ducted through, an outside wall.

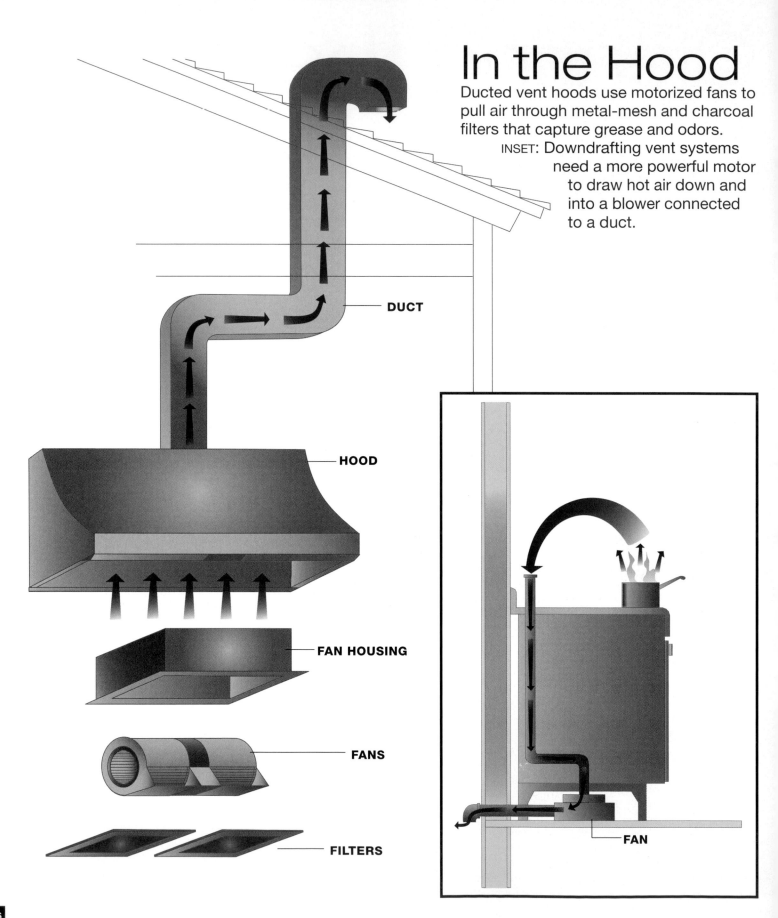

In the Hood

Ducted vent hoods use motorized fans to pull air through metal-mesh and charcoal filters that capture grease and odors.

INSET: Downdrafting vent systems need a more powerful motor to draw hot air down and into a blower connected to a duct.

DUCT

HOOD

FAN HOUSING

FANS

FILTERS

FAN

Because of its prominent placement in the center of the kitchen, an island vent hood can be treated like a piece of sculpture.

To work properly, a hood should span the entire cooktop, and be installed at the right height—about 30 to 36 inches off the range is a good rule," says Tom. "You don't want it too low, or you'll be hitting your head. And you don't want it too high, or it won't catch as much grease." Equally important is making sure it has the might to match your range. A vent's power is measured in CFM (cubic feet per minute); how much you'll need depends on the heat output of your cooktop. The best way to calculate the appropriate CFM is to take the range's total Btu output, as if everything were turned on, and divide by 100. "In other words, calculate according to the worst case," says Ed Gober, national sales manager for Vent-A-Hood. "During the holidays when you're doing a lot of heavy cooking, you probably will need it."

If the distance between your hood and cooktop is greater than the recommended limits, a higher CFM can compensate. Downdraft systems, which are installed or factory-built into a stove or cooktop, can also benefit from additional sucking power since they're battling that law of physics that says hot air rises. However, there is no hard-and-fast rule for how much capacity to add in either case. Steve Thomas, who co-wrote a book on kitchens, opted for the visually unobtrusive downdraft system in his own kitchen, where the cooktop is on a peninsula. A slim, motorized vent rises 10 inches out of the countertop with the flip of a switch but otherwise remains out of the way. "It's not as efficient as a hood would be, but it works fine," he says.

A venting system with too much capacity has its own problems. At the same time it's sucking up grease, a too-powerful fan can also remove a house's heated or cooled air, or, in tightly insulated homes, suck the smoke down a chimney or the exhaust gases from a furnace or water heater into living space. As a rule, kitchen ventilation must go hand in hand with well-balanced whole-house ventilation.

Kitchen ventilation works best, of course, when it is left on throughout the cooking process. But many people don't turn it on because of the noise. "Nobody wants to hear a jet engine taking off in their kitchen," says Jennifer Capasso, brand manager for Thermador. Although some low-end hoods do sound as if their motors were made by Boeing, better-made models at low speeds are as quiet as a murmur. To compare noise output, ask for the units' sone ratings; the lower the better. A husky, commercial-size system can be made quieter by locating the motor on the roof or outside on a wall. "It costs more to install, but if sound is an issue, it's worth it," says Capasso.

Regardless of which system is installed, it must be cleaned regularly. The wire mesh filters snap out and go into the dishwasher, while charcoal filters in ductless models must be replaced periodically according to the manufacturer's recommendations. If grease is allowed to build up on filters, it not only reduces a blower's efficiency but also allows more oily aerosols into the ductwork, creating a fire hazard. (Tom Silva once had to replace an entire roof because grease in the ducting caught fire.) Some hoods have no filters at all; they use centrifugal force to trap grease in a housing that's simply wiped clean with a paper towel.

As costs go up—to more than $30,000 for brass or copper hoods—so do the number of features, and accessories, including slide-out visors that disappear when not in use, heat lamps and warming shelves, pot and utensil racks, adjustable speeds, even sensors that turn the fan on automatically when they sense heat. Ultimately, at a certain price level, hoods are not just about noise or CFM, they're about making a design statement. "High-end hoods add a lot to a kitchen," says Steve. "Some people just have them because they look great." So much for catching grease. ■

Materials

&Surfaces

GOOD LOOKS AND LONG LIFE FOR A GREAT KITCHEN

YOU CAN SOLVE EVERY FLOOR-PLAN PROBLEM. YOU CAN LAVISH attention on style. You can even buy the best cooking equipment. But if you choose a flooring or countertopmaterial that's wrong for how you live, some of the pleasure of owning your new kitchen will vaporize like water splattered on a hot griddle. These surfaces get rough use and plenty of it, so think about the choices carefully. If your floor is hard to clean, or if it has to be treated with kid gloves to look nice, these flaws will face you every time you use the room. Eventually, you'll remodel again just to fix the problems.

What suits other rooms won't necessarily survive in a kitchen, where frequent cleanings are common and sanitary conditions are essential. On the following pages you'll find an unusual variety of materials. One of them (or more) will be just right for your next kitchen.

Not Just Ceramic

Searching for the perfect tile? Consider glass, precious stone, or synthetics, too

THE HARDEST PART OF TILING ANY SURFACE MAY BE THE first step: choosing the tile. Today, even the smallest specialty shops offer everything from intricate mosaics composed of brightly glazed ½-inch squares to hefty 2-foot slabs in earthy terra-cotta tones.

Some of the best-selling ceramics resemble stone. Like the real thing, they make floors look elegant and stay cool underfoot. Unlike most stone, though, ceramic is easy to clean and usually needs no sealer. When the glaze contains sand, tiles also become more slip-resistant than smooth stone.

Offering rich patterns, colors, and textures, ceramic tiles transform floors into works of art. Whether they feature a web of surface cracks, ancient Italian designs, or simply convey visual interest through their shape, these clay pieces give the eye a charming place to land. With so many options available, you might want to apply a mix-and-match approach to the selection process: Alternate colors, insert decorative tiles into plain fields, or create ornamental borders. Tile is made for creative minds.

When it comes to floors, picking a tile requires an eye for more than just style. There are some practical issues to mull over, too. What is the risk that people will slip and fall? Robin Gray, showroom manager at Ann Sacks Tile & Stone in Seattle, says that people tend to worry about slip resistance mostly for bathrooms, but kitchens deserve special attention, too, as do mudrooms and entryways. "People naturally take small steps in a bathroom," Gray says. "Kitchens are larger. Kids are more likely to run in them." Glossy tile can be quite slippery, especially when wet. Matte finishes, glazes with sand in them, and embossed decorations all add traction. And small tiles are inherently more slip-resistant than large ones simply because of the additional grout lines.

Will the tile scratch? Ceramic is harder than most other flooring, but some tiles are tougher than others. The Porcelain Enamel Institute specifies six (0–5) categories of resistance to surface abrasion, with Group 1 surfaces limited to "light duty" on walls, Group 3 for use on floors, and Group 5 for heavy-traffic areas. The American Society for Testing and Materials (ASTM) uses the Mohs scale, which ranks surfaces according to whether they can be scratched by 10 different minerals. Vinyl ranks about 1 because it can be scratched by talc, the softest test mineral. Glazes on wall tiles typically rank 5 or 6; the glaze for tiles used

Since the Spanish colonial era, wealthy families in Mexico have brightened their kitchens with Talavera-style tiles.

on a floor should rank 7, the same as quartz, which is common in sand. Glazed tile often shows scratches more than unglazed tile because the ceramic color underneath shows through.

Will the tile chip if something heavy drops on it? There's an industry measure for this, too, and it ranks tiles in terms of the number of pounds of pressure they can withstand per square inch. The ASTM sets the bar at 90 pounds for wall tiles and 250 pounds for floor tiles. Porcelain tiles, made with finely ground clay baked at high temperatures, are especially tough.

CHOOSING TILE TYPES

What type of tile do you want for your floor? Here's the short course on ceramic tile types:

Bicottura: Made with the traditional process of firing wet clay, then glazing and firing again, sometimes repeatedly. This allows for intricate, multicolored tiles and rich tones. But because of multiple firings, the tile may be too fragile for heavy traffic areas.

Bisque: An unglazed tile.

Crazed: The glaze contains fine cracks, either from age or as an intentional effect; this doesn't compromise strength.

Encaustic: Pattern pressed into the clay and filled with glaze that contrasts the color of the unglazed tile around it; invented during the medieval period and revived during the Victorian era.

Extruded: Clay that is forced through a mold, then cut to size, resulting in a sturdy, consistently shaped tile.

Hand-molded: Identifiable by irregular surfaces and edges—even fingerprints—though this tile is sometimes replicated by machines.

Intaglio: Decorated with impressions in the surface, from leaves and shells to buttons.

Monocottura: A modern process of firing wet clay and glaze simultaneously, resulting in a stronger glazing bond than multifired tiles.

Mosaic: Tile mosaics date back to at least 3000 B.C., when painted clay fragments were hand-laid into mud to create patterns. Today, though, mosaics—whether multicolored or all-white arrays—can be purchased in prearranged sections backed by mesh for ease of installation. They consist typically consist of tiny square, round, or octagonal tiles less than an inch in diameter.

Porcelain: A dry powdered clay that's pressed into shape and fired at high temperatures, resulting in a very durable tile. Not always white, it's used to simulate stone, marble, and terrazzo.

Relief: The design elements project slightly from the surface of the tile.

RIGHT: **From a quarry in southern France comes a unique addition to the list of counter materials: lava. The dull brownish stone, mined from a dormant volcano, is glossed over with impermeable glazes to create a surface that looks like one piece of brilliantly colored tile.**

TOP: Glass mosaic tiles have been made for centuries in Italy, but are still fairly rare in the U.S. These are made from 85 percent recycled glass.

RIGHT: Tiles like these, made with semiprecious stones, were often used in the palaces of Europe during the 12th and 13th centuries. Now you too can walk on floors decorated with lapis lazuli, malachite, onyx, and red jasper. BOTTOM: These Granirex tiles are made of quartz and pigmented epoxy, bonded together with high pressure and then baked. They're more durable than granite.

Screen-printed: Stenciled glaze allows for nearly photographic detail.

Terra-cotta: An unglazed, earthen-red tile; its color varies depending on its source.

Through-body: Unglazed porcelain with uniform composition throughout so that the appearance doesn't change as the surface wears.

TILE TIPS

In terms of design, tiles are either field tiles (those set in the main field of an installation) or trim tiles (those shaped to form a border around the main field; bullnose tiles are one example). Most tile makers offer a range of trim tiles designed to be used with their field tiles. It is almost impossible to get a trim tile from one manufacturer to match a field tile from another, so it's best to work with what's available in one line.

When ordering, bring a measured drawing of the areas to be tiled so a dealer can help design the installation, ensuring that the trim tiles cover the corners and meet the edges properly. The dealer will estimate the number of tiles needed, adding at least 5 percent to provide extras for cutting. Anything left after the job should be packed away carefully and saved for future repairs.

Most tile is laid with uniform spacing between each tile. Some tiles have built-in self-spacing lugs on the edges, which predetermine the width of the joint. Where lugs are absent, tiny plastic Xs called spacers may be used to determine spacing—the spacers are removed once the tile has set. Of course, any tilesetter worthy of the title will have a toolbag full of setting tricks.

Flooring Choices

The possibilities are almost limitless

A KITCHEN FLOOR IS A MOST ABUSED SURFACE. SPLASHED with acidic liquids and stomped on by the grit-encrusted pitter patter of every family foot, kitchens are the New York City of flooring applications: If floors can make it here, they can make it anywhere. But oh, the choices. Here's a hit list to help you sort the options.

Hardwood. Warm underfoot, solid wood isn't as uncomfortable to walk on as harder materials. Polyurethane finishes resist stains and water damage, but in a high-traffic kitchen, frequent refinishing may be required. And as the floor expands and contracts, dirt can collect in cracks. Leaks, or water left on the floor, can do permanent damage.

Ceramic and stone tile. Impervious to dents, these tiles are available in a vast number of colors and patterns. Tiles are often set in thinset adhesive over cement backerboard. Gaps between tiles must be filled with cement-based grout (standard) or epoxy-based grout (expensive but stainproof). The surface is cool, hard, and noisy. Light-colored grouts can show dirt quickly.

Linoleum. This inherently hygienic material can be laid in sheets by contractors, but homeowners can install linoleum tiles with ease. For more on linoleum, see page 126.

Vinyl tile. These flexible tiles offer a wide range of color and pattern options. They are simple to install, although patterns call for careful planning. The many seams between tiles can admit water, however.

Sheet vinyl. The 12-ft.-wide sheets drastically reduce the number of seams, and in many cases eliminate seams altogether. Many colors and patterns are available, but the material is challenging for homeowners to install and requires a very smooth subfloor. Sheet vinyl is an inexpensive floor surface. Like vinyl tile, it can be cut or sliced accidentally by sharp objects.

Cork tile. Laid like vinyl tile, cork is soft underfoot and offers good insulation against noise transmission. Unfinished cork requires frequent sweeping. If you seal the cork, finishes must be reapplied regularly. The color options are limited, too.

Terrazzo. This very durable floor is a mix of marble chips in a cement or resin base. The mix is blended and poured into place over a concrete or plywood subfloor (depending on the base). The surface is then ground smooth, a process that is extremely messy. It can be hard to locate installers.

Rubber. This durable floor is almost maintenance-free, which is why you'll find it so often in commercial applications. It is laid like vinyl, in sheets or as tiles. It is comfortable underfoot, resists

HARDWOOD

LAMINATE

CORK

LINOLEUM

spills, and offers many textures, but has a somewhat industrial look.

Carpeting. Carpeting is soft underfoot, quick to install, and easily replaced. But in a kitchen it may retain odors from cooking or spills, and is distinctly unhygienic.

Epoxy. Squeegied or rolled into place by professional installers, epoxy provides a durable, seamless surface. It may be tough to find experienced installation craftsmen, however.

Engineered wood. A plywood substrate topped with a thin layer of solid wood and a tough, factory-applied finish make this a durable option for kitchens. For more, see pages 128 and 168.

Laminate flooring. Often confused with engineered wood flooring, these planks get their appearance from a photographic image of wood. Glued to a fiberboard core, the picture is protected by a clear coating. The planks can be glued together edge to edge, and are highly water-resistant if properly installed. Similar to the plastic laminate on your countertops, laminate flooring is more scratch-resistant than any wood floor. However, once it does scratch, the damage is permanent.

VINYL

Linoleum Lives On

A fresh look at Grandma's kitchen floor

FOR LINOLEUM MAKERS, IT'S SOMETHING OF A bittersweet joke: A man walks into a flooring store and says he wants to buy linoleum for his kitchen. "No problem," says the store clerk, leading him to racks of vinyl flooring samples.

"It's amazing," says Frank O'Neill, publisher of *Floor Focus* magazine. "Even dealers you'd think would know better use the words vinyl and linoleum interchangeably." In truth, the two couldn't be more different. Vinyl flooring is a synthetic product made of chlorinated petrochemicals; linoleum is produced entirely from natural ingredients. Vinyl will melt if a lighted match or cigarette lands on it; linoleum can't. And most vinyl patterns are printed into the product's surface; linoleum's colors go all the way through. "As linoleum wears, different layers of color are gradually revealed," says Duo Dickinson, an architect in Madison, Connecticut, who has also used the material on backsplashes and countertops. "It can be quite beautiful." Durability is another of linoleum's attributes; some floors have survived 30 to 40 years in tough commercial environments. "It seems to last forever," Dickinson says.

Amazingly, linoleum's makeup and manufacture have hardly changed since an Englishman named Frederick Walton patented the product in 1863. The story goes that he got the idea from the leathery skin of oxidized linseed oil that forms on paint. Walton eventually perfected a mix of linseed oil, cork dust, wood flour, tree resins, ground limestone, and pigments—the same recipe used by linoleum makers today—and figured out how to press it onto a jute backing. Then he gave his concoction its name, combining the Latin words for flax (linum), the source of linseed oil, and oil (oleum).

Made in sheets, tiles, or even decorative area "rugs" and stuck to the floor with adhesive, linoleum became a favorite floor-covering in stores, restaurants, and kitchens, where its smooth, water-resistant surface made cleaning less of a chore. But when cheaper vinyl flooring became available in 1947, people began turning away from drab, old-fashioned linoleum.

But now linoleum is surging back. The Dutch linoleum maker Forbo Industries, which commands most of the U.S. linoleum market, has seen sales jump. Domco, a Canadian maker of vinyl flooring, plunged into linoleum in 1997 in response to requests from architects and specifiers. That same year, in what many see as the surest sign of linoleum's renewed popularity, vinyl-flooring giant Armstrong bought the world's second-largest linoleum maker, DLW (Deutsche Linoleum Werke), reentering a market it had left for dead in the 1970s.

Why the renewed interest? Color, for one thing. Today,

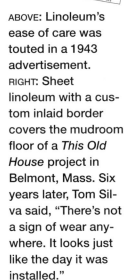

ABOVE: Linoleum's ease of care was touted in a 1943 advertisement.
RIGHT: Sheet linoleum with a custom inlaid border covers the mudroom floor of a *This Old House* project in Belmont, Mass. Six years later, Tom Silva said, "There's not a sign of wear anywhere. It looks just like the day it was installed."

linoleum comes in a Crayola box of vibrant hues, a far cry from the muddy offerings available before World War II. And new factory-applied sealer coats protect those colors against dirt and stains.

No matter its color, a growing number of architects and designers regard linoleum as environmentally friendly. "From a resource standpoint, it's great," says *Environmental Building News* editor Alex Wilson, who installed a linoleum floor in the kitchen and bath area at the newsletter's offices in Brattleboro, Vermont. "It's made from natural, largely renewable, materials, and there are no environmental toxins involved in its manufacturing or disposal," says Wilson.

It's also a natural choice for vintage houses. Dean and Lauren Gallant—owners of an old house in Belmont, Massachusetts, that *This Old House* renovated in 1993—put linoleum in their laundry room, mudroom, and one of the bathrooms. "The original butler's pantry had it, and the flooring was still in reasonably good shape," says Dean Gallant. "So we said, 'Well, if it lasted that long, why not do it again?'"

Of course, linoleum does have its drawbacks. Because it's porous, its appearance and continued resilience depend on regular maintenance. Walt Bamonto, owner of Merlin Flooring in Farmington, New York, advises that new floors be given one or two coats of acrylic sealer and a recoat once a year after that to keep them looking fresh. Also, newly laid linoleum floors have a pronounced linseed-oil scent. This dissipates in a matter of months, but bothers some people in the meantime. Even so, retail stores, day-care centers, and hospitals remain prime buyers of the flooring because of its natural bactericidal qualities.

In the view of interior designer Sue Walling, of SW Design Inc. in Minneapolis, linoleum's pluses outweigh its minuses, particularly in kitchens. "Linoleum is comfortable to walk on, you can get it wet, and you don't have to worry about dropping knives on it, the way you do with most vinyl." (To make a gash in linoleum disappear, it can be filled with a mix of wood glue and fine scrapings off a leftover piece.)

Walling admits, however, that clients are often reluctant to go with linoleum, even though sheet linoleum costs about the same (including installation) as vinyl sheet flooring, and remains a bargain compared to ceramic tile or wood. She thinks their reluctance stems from perceptions anchored in the past. But those perceptions seem to be be changing. According to Walling, "Once you show people what linoleum looks like and how it holds up, they really love it."

ABOVE: Tom Silva demonstrates how to use a hard-rubber J-roller to press down seams. Here he's working on a border stripe, a contrasting color inlaid into a sheet of linoleum. BELOW: Modern linoleum spans the color spectrum. One company makes sheets and tile in 147 different shades, both marbled, as shown here, and solid.

Floor in A Flash

Prefinished and uniform, engineered wood floors install quickly

ENGINEERED FLOORING SEEMS LIKE IT OUGHT TO BE cheaper than solid wood. After all, the tongue-and-groove strips are made from plywood, with only the surface layer (called the wear layer) cut from maple, oak, cherry, or some other hardwood. But manufactured planks can cost just as much as, or even more than, their solid-wood counterparts. Still, engineered flooring products are chosen for 40 percent of new wood floors.

What's the appeal? Imagine moving out of the family room for only 12 hours as a contractor pulls up the old wall-to-wall carpeting, then cuts and assembles prefinished boards. No sanding, no waiting for multiple coats of polyurethane to dry. The floor is complete as soon as the boards are installed. And unlike solid-wood floors, these floors can be laid directly over most substrates, including concrete. And over a wood subfloor, the strips are readily installed by homeowners (see page 168). The

Using a special pneumatic stapler, installer Jeff Hosking quickly lays a prefinished engineered wood floor. Some floors can be installed without fasteners; instead, edges are glued together.

1. Solid-oak flooring has a thick wear layer (the wood above the tongue) and can be sanded frequently, but the material expands and contracts seasonally. 2. This five-ply plank has a 1/16-in. wear layer—not enough to sand. Engineered flooring products offer dimensional stability, but wear layer thicknesses vary. 3. Some engineered planks imitate narrow strip flooring. 4. Planks that are 3/8 in. thick must be nailed in place. 5. Those with a 9/16-in. total thickness can be floated (installed without nailing). 6. These six-ply boards have a hefty 3/8-in. birch layer; note the microbeveled edges.

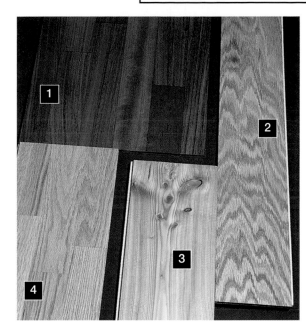

RIGHT: Foreign and domestic hardwoods are readily available in various widths of engineered planks:

1. Flat-cut Brazilian cherry.
2. Rotary-cut red oak.
3. Flat-cut larch pine.
4. Flat-cut oak. (This plank contains strips of three different widths.)

Engineered flooring varies in its durability. Inexpensive products may have a wear layer just $\frac{1}{10}$ inch-thick, and cannot be sanded if the finish has to be replaced. Premium products have a thick wear layer and can withstand as many as five sandings, extending the life of the flooring. Solid-wood flooring, by comparison, can endure as many as seven careful sandings.

Consider, too, what's under that top veneer. The tongue-and-groove board should contain at least three plies in all, but five is better, says Jeff Hosking, a hardwood flooring expert. "The more plies, the more stable the floor will be," he says. Stability means that joints won't open up in dry winter weather. The center core should also be made of solid wood such as poplar, rather than a cheaper composite material, to provide a more stable base and a slight spring underfoot like solid wood.

Prefinished engineered floors aren't quite as even as floors that are sanded in place, says Don Dickel, a third-generation wood-floor installer and finisher in Bangor, Maine. To hide slight differences in board thickness, some manufacturers mill a microbevel along each edge, which creates shallow grooves between planks.

The factory finish on engineered flooring is very durable. Aluminum oxide coatings are the toughest of all. This superhard powder is added to a urethane finish. Manufacturers guarantee aluminum oxide finishes for 25 years (versus a likely life of 10 years for three coats of polyurethane). But Hosking has read the fine print: "It means that in 25 years there will still be something to protect the wood from water," he says. "But no finish is scratch-proof or dent-proof."

flooring can even be floated over a $\frac{1}{8}$-inch plastic foam-insulation pad. "That," says Tom Silva, "makes things quieter downstairs." But the biggest appeal is to homeowners living in the midst of renovations—engineered floors go down quick. That, in part, is why *This Old House* chose engineered floors for the Santa Barbara, Milton, and Watertown projects.

Not all engineered flooring effectively mimics solid wood. The key is whether the wear layer is rotary-cut or flat-cut. Rotary-cutting generates wide sheets of veneer with the same distinctive, repeating grain pattern of plywood. Flat-cut veneer, on the other hand, comes from a slice made directly along a log's length. The result looks more like solid wood, but is more costly to make.

Countertop Choices

Gleaming steel, rustic stone, and a host of other design possibilities

RECENTLY, ALL SORTS OF NEW MATERIALS, COLORS, and finishes have made their way onto kitchen cabinets. In fact, there's no reason to limit yourself to one or the other—many kitchens feature a combination of countertop materials, each selected for a particular quality. As the choices broaden, surface character and texture are becoming critical elements of the design. A kitchen is considered a wet area, which means that the countertop must be carefully chosen and installed to resist spills. With so many materials to choose from, that won't be a problem.

Ceramic tile. Available in an enormous variety of colors, textures, and patterns, glazed ceramic tile is water-resistant and durable. However, some maintenance is required: Grout must be sealed (and usually resealed every few years) and care must be taken to avoid dropping heavy objects that can break the tile. The good news: A broken tile can be replaced without disturbing the entire counter surface. Handmade and hand-decorated tile are much more expensive than machine-made tile, and often more fragile too. For cost savings, consider decorative edge tiles combined with plainer tiles in the field (the large center area of an installation).

Butcher block. Hardwood strips (usually maple, beech, or oak) cut in even or varying lengths are glued and laminated under pressure to make butcher block. The surface can be oiled or sealed, but sealed block should not be used as a cutting surface. The block will show wear and tear, but because it's meant to be a functional work surface, these marks should be seen as an asset rather than a liability. More severe damage or stains can be removed with fine-grit sandpaper. If used as a food-prep surface, butcher block must be cleaned thoroughly and disinfected after each use, particularly after raw meat has been cut on it.

Solid surfacing. A synthetic, nonporous plastic-and-mineral compound that is repairable (small scratches, burns, and serious stains can be buffed or sanded out and repolished). Seams are joined with a color-tinted adhesive, which becomes invisible when sanded. Solid-surface counters are available in high

The extraordinary variety of countertop choices is evident from the photos at right. To make your decision even harder, every countertop material can be used to create a backsplash. If you mix dissimilar materials, however, pay close attention to the joint where they meet. Materials that expand and contract at different rates may cause a gap to open between them.

CERAMIC TILE

SOLID SURFACING

CONCRETE

STAINLESS STEEL

BUTCHER BLOCK

SOLID SURFACING: NEW COUNTER IN AN HOUR

Because so much of the work has been done in the shop, installing a solid-surface countertop in the home is speedy and simple. Installers Doug Ward and George Moreo heft a one-piece, 200-pound counter with an integral sink atop the cabinets. **(1)** Once the counter is in place, Ward drills the faucet openings in the sink top with a hole saw. A plumber will come in later to hook up the fixtures and drain. **(2)** While Moreo lifts the countertop, Ward guns a thin bead of silicone between the top and the cabinets, locking the top into place. **(3)** To allow the solid-surfacing to expand and contract with temperature changes, installers must leave a 1/16-inch space between the countertop and surrounding walls. Ward seals the gap with silicone. From start to finish, the entire process takes about an hour.

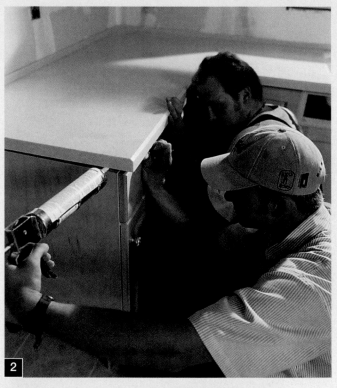

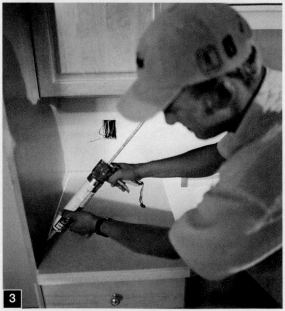

gloss or matte finishes, but a hot pan can scorch either one. The color palette is vast, but neutrals predominate; plain blacks and whites are the big winners. Most companies sell solid surfacing only through factory-certified fabricators. A lower-cost look-alike is solid-surface veneer. Just ⅛ inch thick, it is attached to fiberboard and performs similarly to solid surfacing at about half the cost.

Plastic laminates. Once the standard surface for a modern kitchen, laminates are available in literally hundreds of colors, patterns, and textures. Laminate countertops are inexpensive, durable, and easy to maintain. But they are not heatproof, their seams are vulnerable to water intrusion, and scratches and burns cannont be repaired. A standard sheet of laminate is less than 1/16 inch thick, and is bonded to a plywood or fiberboard substrate using contact adhesive.

Concrete. Cast concrete is a relatively new surface material for kitchens. It varies widely in texture, finish, and appearance because each countertop is individually crafted and colored. Concrete can be installed in seamless slabs (see page 138), and in a kitchen, the finish should be renewed on a regular basis.

Natural stone. Countertop stones include granite, marble, limestone, slate, and soapstone. The broad range of colors, grains, finishes, and textures available makes stone suitable for any decorating scheme. Slabs are generally available in four- to eight-foot lengths; the larger and thicker the slab, the costlier (and more labor-intensive) the countertop. Be aware that joints will show. Some stone, particularly marble (see box at right), is quite porous; a special sealant may be required. One cost-saving strategy is to purchase 21- or 24-inch square stone tiles, rather than slabs. That approach can turn an only-for-professionals project into do-it-yourself work.

Unlike marble and granite, soapstone has a crystalline structure that allows it to heat and cool thousands of times without cracking. It comes in hues ranging from white to gray, green, or brown, but only gray stone is used for countertops.

Stainless steel. This durable metal can withstand almost any abuse without rusting or discoloring. However, it will show surface abrasions, can be dented, and may be noisy to work on. Stainless is measured by gauge; the higher the gauge number, the thinner the material (18 to 14 gauge is typical for countertops). Most stainless countertops are custom-fabricated, but check with restaurant-supply houses for ready-made units that might fit your plan. For more on stainless steel, see page 140.

USING OLD MARBLE

"Marble's not a great choice for most kitchen countertops because it's porous and stains easily," says Tom Silva. But this piece of paint-splattered marble, salvaged from a basement worktable, was cleaned up and put to good use on the top of a slender kitchen peninsula. The rough-hewn quarry edge of one side shows traces of its tainted past. Here's how one stone expert would clean the paint-covered slab:

1. Remove the paint with a razor and regular paint solvent.

2. Sand the entire surface wet with 120-grit paper by hand or with a random-orbit sander, not a beltsander.

3. Finish up with 400-grit paper, again wet.

4. Use a penetrating sealer that contains silicone. Don't use oil—it attracts dirt and can darken marble.

Counter Intelligence

Solid surfacing can be a smart choice

EVEN BEFORE *THE GRADUATE*'S BEN BRADDOCK was told to look for his future in plastics, DuPont chemist Don Slocum had a polymer vision of his own. In late 1963, Slocum and a band of fellow scientists were assigned to find uses for the company's plastic technologies in the nation's kitchens and bathrooms. Working in a makeshift lab in an abandoned Delaware tire plant, they combined DuPont's acrylic resins with a filler to create a new kind of countertop material that was repairable, stain- and germ-resistant, and solid, unlike the popular laminates adhered to particleboard. "We knew right away we had something special," remembers Slocum, who named the new product Corian, after his daughter Carrie Ann.

Did they ever. Thirty-four years later, solid surfacing (the generic name for Slocum's creation) has become a billion-dollar business. The National Kitchen and Bath Association has reported that solid surfacing is the countertop covering of choice in a great many kitchens, beating out marble, granite, tile and plastic laminates. "The factories can't even keep up with countertop demand," says Mike Duggan, editor of *SolidSurface* magazine, the industry's trade journal. "Everyone is in full production," he adds.

Although DuPont Corian still rules a large percentage of the solid surface industry, since Slocum's original patent ran out in the mid 1980s four other national brands—Avonite, Wilsonart's Gibraltar, Nevamar's Fountainhead, and Formica's Surell (along with some 160 regional manufacturers) pushed into the market. The bulk of the business is still countertops, but the material is also turning up in everything from furniture and flooring to golf clubs and pet bowls.

So what is solid surfacing? Essentially, it's a combination of two ingredients: a filler, most often alumina trihydrate (ATH, a white powder refined from bauxite ore), and a clear resin binder, (either acrylic or polyester or a mixture of the two). The colors and speckles are created by adding pigments and tiny bits of the finished product itself. When filler and binder come into contact, they chemically meld into a solid that's waterproof, fire-resistant, UV-resistant, and hard enough to resist denting and chipping, yet forgiving enough to be shaped and finished with carbide-tipped woodworking tools.

The same chemical reaction can be used to join pieces together with virtually invisible seams, making possible accent edges, inlays, and completely integral sinks and backsplashes. To make an inlay, a fabricator routs a design into the surfacing, then squeezes colored resin into the depressions. After the resin cures, the surface is sanded smooth. The

This one-piece stretch of solid-surface countertop, including an integral sink, weighs a hefty but manageable 200 lbs. The two lengths of countertop and the sink were glued together with a two-part adhesive that, when sanded, makes seams invisible.

For this beach-house kitchen, solid-surface countertops offer durability approaching that of granite, but without the formality.

Solid surfacing with a matching backsplash makes a countertop seem larger than it really is. Edges can be shaped as readily as solid wood.

process is time-consuming and expensive, but when worked up by a creative craftsman, the results can be dazzling.

Being nonporous, solid surfacing resists stains, mold, and bacterial growth. And because it is the same material throughout, small scratches and scorch marks can be buffed out with fine sandpaper or a Scotch-Brite–type pad.

Still, solid surfacing isn't kryptonite. For all its good looks and easy care, it is, after all, a plastic; it doesn't have the heat resistance of granite or ceramic tile. While brief contact with a hot saucepan isn't likely to cause damage, prolonged exposure can leave an indelible white scorch mark (which can be fixed with a patch), or cause the counter to crack. "It sounds like a shot when it cracks," says Ed Wright, owner of INcounters, in Abilene, Texas. Like most fabricators, Wright routinely leaves a piece of left-over countertop with the consumer so any future repairs will be color-matched. "Solid surfacing expands and contracts based on temperature the way wood does in contact with water," Wright says. "You have to treat it very carefully when it comes to heat."

It isn't cheap, either. Countertops cost between $100 and $150 a linear foot installed, about three times the cost of plastic laminate and about the same as granite or marble. If you add the inegral solid-surface sink—as most consumers do—the cost jumps another $600 to $800. Even so, fabricators say they're serving more middle-income clients. "It used to be a product reserved for the high-end homeowners; now people in less expensive homes are demanding it," says Wright. "They say, 'My friend has it; my neighbor has it . . . that's what I want.'"

Some manufacturers hope to win even more converts with products like ⅛-inch-thick solid-surface veneer. Applied over fiberboard and seamed with the same adhesive, the veneers have the appearance and features of solid surfacing—including integral sinks—at considerably less cost. "As far as looks and performance, it's the same," says Alison DeMartino, public relations manager for Wilsonart, which introduced the Gibraltar solid-surface veneer nationally in 1986. "The only difference is you can't do some of the high-end features, like routed-in drainboards, carved edges, and inlays."

Though he has yet to use it, Tom thinks solid-surfacing veneer could be "a great choice for someone who can't afford regular solid surfacing." Still, some who work with full-thickness solid surfacing remain wary of the newcomers. "It ought to be less expensive—it's less material," says INcounters's Wright. "Logic tells you that if it's ⅛ inch thick, it's not going to perform the same as ½-inch-thick material."

Fabricators also disagree over the merits of the various brands as well. Although they look and cost about the same, there are some significant chemical differences in their makeup. Some use an acrylic resin as their binder. Others use polyester, or a poly/acrylic blend. Avonite has a product that omits the ATH filler altogether in favor of pure polyester resin, which permits strikingly deep, near translucent colors and larger chips of color. Other fabricators say the acrylic-based products, while not as lustrous, are stronger and easier to work with. Polyester resists acetone and citric acids better than acrylics, but it has no ATH, which acts as a fire retardant, so it can burn.

So how to choose? Often it comes down to aesthetics. Solid white, the most popular color, is also the least expensive and the least likely to show

The subtle colorations possible with solid surfacing often serve as a foil to bolder materials, such as this ceramic-tile backsplash.

scratches, at least until dirt gets in. Speckles, on the other hand, camouflage smudges and crumbs. "They're all basically the same material," says fabricator Dani Homrich, of Dani Designs in Rochester Hills, Michigan. "Pick a color you're going to love living with."

And pick a good countertop fabricator. Most manufacturers of solid surfacing require fabricators to be certified before allowing them to work with and install a particular product. (Some warranties cover installation; others do not.) That's

This countertop and back-splash are inset with contrasting colors. The ability to incorporate intricate details, particularly at edges, is common to all solid surfacing.

why manufacturers would rather not have home-owners fabricating their own countertops (some manufacturers even prohibit it). And although DuPont Corian does offer some prefab vanity tops and shower stalls, most consumers still turn the work over to professional fabrication companies. "We've found we can make a custom top for about the same price a do-it-yourselfer would pay for a stock top," says INcounters's Ed Wright, "and when you're spending that kind of money, you want it done right."

The Perfect Countertop?

Poured concrete looks good and lasts forever

UNTIL YOU'VE SEEN ONE, A COUNTERTOP MADE OF concrete seems an odd proposition. Countertops are one of a kitchen's most visible elements, and on the building material glamour meter, concrete ranks just above the wax ring under a toilet. We're happy to have good, gray concrete undergirding our houses, but pouring it atop expensive cabinetry seems like a misbegotten design statement, industrial chic pushed to ugly excess.

Yet concrete is in many ways the ideal countertop material: durable, seamless, and aesthetically versatile. Concrete can mimic mineral slabs ranging from veined marble to lustrous obsidian, or it can strike out in more daring directions—anyone for a maroon kitchen island shaped like a football? And the cost of a completed concrete countertop can beat the installed prices of materials such as solid surfacing and granite.

Carol Orr wanted concrete's massive, textured presence after ogling some countertops in upscale interior design magazines. "We like unusual things," she says, "and concrete was definitely original." So she commissioned Manuel Mercado, of North Texas Bomanite, an architectural concrete company, to begin the weeklong process of installing 140 square feet—more than a ton—of concrete in the galley kitchen of her rambling contemporary.

Mercado usually makes countertops in his company's workshop and brings the finished slabs to a kitchen. But when countertops are longer than 10 feet or include cutouts for sinks or a cooktop, they must be built on site.

Site-built concrete countertops start with a form, and a form starts with a bottom. To make one for the kitchen's center island, Mercado and his assistant, carpenter Eusevio Martinez, cut plywood to cover the cabinets precisely, attaching it with screws. The sides of the forms consist of stiff boards or flexible hardboard strips, depending on whether straight lengths or sinuous curves are called for.

BELOW: Massive yet smooth and soft-edged, the completed countertop is 3 in. thick.
RIGHT: While Eusevio Martinez, left, dumps concrete into the form, Manuel Mercado quickly spreads it over the plywood base. A cooktop and a small round sink will eventually occupy the two cutouts. This 3-by-9-ft. countertop will weigh 700 lbs., but factory-built cabinets can easily carry the load.

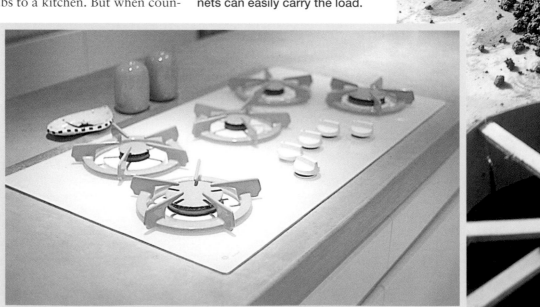

After two days of patient, exacting formwork, Mercado mixes the concrete. He dumps his recipe—5 gallons Type 1 portland cement, 15 gallons sand, and 1¼ gallons of ⅜-inch gravel—into a portable mixer in Orr's driveway. To this, he dribbles in a mixture of 5 gallons water and 1 gallon acrylic concrete-bonding agent. When he can squeeze the mix it into a neat ball that doesn't crumble, it's ready.

The bonding agent is a vital ingredient. Concrete shrinks as it cures, and it tends to crack at stress points, such as the inside corners of openings. The bonding agent and steel reinforcing added later ensure a crack-free countertop.

A wheelbarrow-load at a time, Mercado and Martinez muscle the mix indoors, shovel it into the form, and push it into every corner. They have just 30 minutes before the concrete begins to set. After filling the form about halfway, Mercado adds a layer of galvanized-steel stucco lath, also called diamond mesh, to reinforce the concrete and prevent cracking altogether. To reinforce the 3-inch-wide strip of concrete at the front of the cooktop cutout, Mercado inserts a length of angle iron sized to extend 3 inches beyond each corner, and immediately buries it with more concrete. After filling the entire form, Mercado uses a succession of wood floats and steel trowels to smooth the surface. Then, with an edging tool, he cuts a slight radius into the top edge of the concrete.

Back at the mixing stage, Mercado could have added colorant and given the concrete a uniform hue from top to bottom. But for the textured, mottled look Orr specified, Mercado and Martinez sprinkle two light-colored powders—masonry colorant—on the firm but still wet surface. They work the surface with trowels to meld the two shades.

The next day, the forms are stripped and Mercado finishes the sides. He first paints them with a 50/50 mix of water and bonding agent, then fills any voids with a wet batch of gravel-free portland cement. Next, he trowels on a paste made from equal portions of the two colorants and finishes by wrapping his hand with plastic sheeting, dipping it in water and gently rubbing and smoothing all the edges. After waiting two days for the concrete to cure, Mercado lightly sands the tops and sides to remove stray nubs and whorls, then seals the counters with two coats of low-gloss water-based acrylic sealer.

With the sinks and cooktop reinstalled, Orr is delighted. "It's just what we wanted to contrast with the slick look of the cabinets." And after a couple of weeks cooking, she also finds the countertops eminently practical. "You just can't hurt this stuff."

Heady Metal

Stainless steel, zinc, and copper are the signature surfaces of serious cooks

URBAN PLANNER PHILIP L. Rampulla worked as a chef for six years, so when planning his family's new home, he was serious about the cooking space. "I wanted a chef's kitchen," he says, with a commercial range, plenty of easy-to-reach storage, and great work surfaces. "I'm used to cooking in kitchens that have the right kind of counters," he says, "and that means stainless steel."

Restaurants choose stainless steel for good reasons: It's durable, resilient, easy to clean, and attractive. "You can put a scalding pan directly on the metal," says Randall Sisk, a kitchen designer in Kansas City, Missouri. "And for doughs that need a cool surface, like pastries and dumplings, this is the counter to work on. Best of all, when you're done, you just wipe everything down with soap and water." An alloy of iron, chromium, and nickel, stainless steel is unaffected even by kitchen liquids that react with other metals: lemon juice, vinegar, spaghetti sauce, bleach. About the biggest staining risk is the rust from a wet cast-iron pan or steel-wool pad that's left on the counter overnight. And while steel will scratch slightly from everyday use, you can buy it with a random-grain finish that hides all but the deepest scratches.

The cost of stainless steel is in the same ballpark as other premium countertops like marble and granite, but it has a distinct advantage over these materials: The countertop, backsplash, and sink can be integrated into a single seamless unit. Solid surfacing can accomplish the same feat, but it's considerably heavier than stainless. And also like solid surfacing, stainless steel offers no grooves or caulked joints where dirt can collect or water can seep through. Metal is friendy to crockery and glassware, too. "You have to be careful when you set the crystal on your granite counter, or you might lose a glass," says John Cave, of Quest Metalworks Ltd., a metal countertop fabricator in Vancouver, Canada. "But metal has a bit of spring."

Making stainless-steel countertops requires exact measurements of the kitchen, Cave says, because "unlike other materials, even stone, metal counters can't be adjusted on site." In the shop, metalworkers transfer the dimensions to

ABOVE: A steel-faced cabinet houses cooking utensils right next to the six-burner commercial range. RIGHT: Ash cabinetry and 70 sq. ft. of stainless-steel work surfaces give this kitchen a professional appearance.

18-gauge sheet metal (about 1/20th of an inch thick), then slice it with a shear that looks like a giant paper cutter. The sink opening is carved out with a plasma arc—a high-temperature stream of electricity. Workers use a 12-foot sheet metal brake to fold the edges down and the back-splashes up. The next step, welding the corners together, is "where the real craftsmanship comes in," says Cave. The welds have to be completely free of voids so they can be ground and polished until every surface is smooth and shining, as if it had been poured in place. Then, the top is flipped over and a plywood substrate is contact-cemented to the underside. The entire process takes about eight hours for the average 8-foot-long top with one sink.

A stainless countertop is installed just like any other type: by driving screws up through cleats (strips of wood that run across the top of each cabinet) into the plywood substrate. If the counter is too large to deliver in one piece, the fabricator will come on site to weld sections together and polish the seams.

Not all of the metal countertops that Cave makes are steel, however. Some people forgo its bright, antiseptic character for the older look of copper and zinc. "Long before houses had running water, dry sinks were lined with these metals," says Sisk. Zinc was also common for tabletops, drainboards, and backsplashes in the 19th century. Both metals, which cost about the same as stainless steel for countertops, lend a softer, more traditional appearance to the kitchen. But they also scratch more easily and are prone to buckling slightly if trivets aren't used under hot pans.

Copper and zinc also tarnish. "The look and feel changes constantly," says Gerry Santora, of Soupcan Inc., a metal countertop fabricator in Chicago. "It's very much alive." Keeping a high luster would require almost constant polishing, so most homeowners just clean them with a sponge or wet cloth, allowing the metal to develop a patina: bronzy brown for copper and pewter gray for zinc. "One thing you can't do is spot-polish these metals," says Santora. "The area you clean will stand out like a sore thumb."

For Rampulla, practicality dictated the choice of a countertop. "I've seen a lot of high-end kitchens where the counters look pretty, but they aren't functional." But there's no denying that his gleaming steel counters make a statement about how seriously he takes his cooking. "People always ask me when I'm going to turn this place into a restaurant," he says.

Great Slate

This ancient stone makes a richly textured, durable choice for countertops—and floors

M ENTION SLATE AND PEOPLE THINK OF ROOFING, and for good reason. The material is nearly impervious to rain and snow, invulnerable to the sun's destructive rays or sparks wafting out of a chimney, and graced with uncommon good looks. But because it costs so much more than asphalt shingles, a slate roof is not a common option. Consider this irony, however: For flooring and countertops, slate is a steal. It costs considerably less than granite, marble, or limestone, yet performs as well or better. And slate stands out as something special. "It's textured, not shiny-smooth," says Wade Pierce, of Terrazzo & Stone Supply Co., in Bellevue, Washington. "Our customers love the earth tones it comes in."

Slate is one of only a few rocks that split easily into layers both thin and strong. Many stones with this property are called slate, but true slate, which was formed from tiny particles of clay and silt that drifted to sea bottoms hundreds of millions of years ago, has a fine, smooth texture. Under the heat and pressure of the earth's crust rising into mountain ranges, the deposits were transformed into slate. Bluestone, one of slate's close look-alikes, also formed on ancient seabeds, but is technically a sandstone because it is made of sand-size grains of mineral rock. Even among the true slates, characteristics vary considerably from region to region and quarry to quarry.

For countertops, backsplashes, and floors in a home, the softer stones will hold up just fine. But on a highly trafficked commercial floor, only the hardest slates suit. The American Society for Testing and Materials (ASTM) applies a three-tier ranking (based on laboratory tests), in which S-1 is the best stone and S-3 is the worst. All are equally strong, but the lowest grade absorbs nearly twice as much water and is seven times more susceptible to acid damage than the top grade. For flooring, the most critical factor is abrasion resistance, measured in an open-ended ASTM scale that generally rates slate from 3 to 12. A flooring slate should rate 8 or higher. Slate's density is about the same as other countertop stone: 15 pounds per square foot when cut 1 inch thick.

Slate can be purchased in sizes that range from broad slabs for one-piece countertops to thin, small squares that install like ceramic tile. For flooring, backsplashes, or countertops, it's important to buy gauged slate, which has been ground to a uniform thickness. "It's far easier to set," notes Charlie Helsby, manager of American Slate Co.'s showroom in Seattle. The exposed surface, though, can be left just as it was when the stone was split at the quarry—with a rough striated finish known as natural cleft—or it can be honed flat (the usual finish for countertops).

Green slate serves as the countertop, the flooring, even the sink in this kitchen.

Because slate on a counter or floor is susceptible to staining and scratching, it's generally treated with a protective finish. There are two basic types, sealers and impregnators, each available in oil- and water-based formulas. Sealers coat the surface with a thin layer of acrylic resin. Impregnators, also known as penetrating sealers, partially fill the stone's pores with resin, silicone, or fluoropolymers like Teflon. Sealers are more difficult to maintain: The finish builds up and eventually must be stripped with solvent and a buffing machine. Impregnators don't build up because the surface is sponged off about five minutes after application. Andrew Levine, of Stone Care International, a manufacturer of stone protectants, recommends testing any product in an inconspicuous spot first because it may darken slate. Or leave the stone au naturel. "One of the most beautiful floors I've seen was in a bank in Vermont dating from the 1930s," says Jim Strickland of Maryland Stone Services. "All they had ever done was wash when necessary with diluted Murphy's Oil Soap."

The price of slate varies depending on color, size, finish, and your distance from the quarry. Countertop slabs from ¾ to 1 inch thick typically run $50 to $75 a square foot, including custom cutting and edging but not installation. Flooring tiles start at $2 a square foot. ∎

ABOVE: To create a watertight sink, slate slabs should be joined with grooved channels, epoxy, and screws. The work is not for amateurs.

Basic

Skills

TOOLS AND TECHNIQUES FOR KITCHEN REMODELING

S WEAT EQUITY—INVESTING YOUR SKILLS TO IMPROVE YOUR HOUSE—IS one of the best ways to cut the costs of kitchen remodeling. Accumulating the appropriate skills, however, is a little like stocking a toolbox: You don't have to gather everything you'll ever need at the outset. Instead, gather just what's required for the next project (tools or skills) because you can always add more later. Each completed project will make the next one a bit easier.

A kitchen is the most complicated room in a house, but many of the common skills you'll need to remodel it—figuring layouts, working with wood, cutting tile, soldering pipes—can be built while doing the projects that follow. And though you won't often have to move a window, sometimes that's exactly what will unlock the full potential of your floor plan.

Before Tom Silva's tango with this 80-lb. replacement window, he fastened waterproof splines around the opening, over the building paper. At the bottom of the window, he lapped the splines over the flashing so water will drain away from the wall. The spline at the top of the opening goes on last to overlap the two pieces on the sides. Tom normally tops windows with flashing but not in this case: The overhanging soffit will keep water out.

Working With Windows

In a kitchen, adding (or moving) a window can make a new floor plan possible

THE OLD WHITE-PINE WINDOW WITH ITS HAND-PLANED muntins and peg-joined sash had withstood the assault of snow, rain, ice, and wind for about 270 years. But by the time *This Old House* contractor Tom Silva found it, the wood was beyond repair and there was no way he could reuse the window in the house he was remodeling. It simply had to be replaced.

When functioning properly, a window lets in the best of the outdoors in the form of light and fresh air. When a window fails, it lets in too much of the outdoors—not only cold winter drafts but also water. Moisture seeping in from the outside or condensing on cold surfaces inside can deteriorate a window frame. If unchecked, this will destroy the structural integrity of a wall. "You can replace the sash alone," says Tom, but he recommends taking that course only if frames and sills are still square and in good condition. "If you find any rot, the entire window unit should be removed and replaced."

At a *This Old House* project in Milton, Massachusetts, Tom was able to save nine early-Georgian windows in the front to "keep the feel of the house," he says. But the few remaining original windows in the back had become lost in a hodgepodge of tacked-on additions, so replacing them with new, energy-efficient ones made sense.

Once he removed the sash and tore out the old window frames, Tom inspected the studs. (Had they not been sound, he would have replaced them.) He measured the rough openings, from stud to stud and from header to rough sill, and ordered suitable replacements. When the windows arrived four weeks later with weatherstripped preprimed sash mounted in the jambs, they were ready to pop in.

Well, almost. First, like any good window installer, Tom had to detail the opening to keep water out, keep heat in and make sure the unit looked its best inside and out.

TOP: Wooden windows last longer with one moisture-repellent coat of oil-based primer on the back of the casing. Priming protects the wood from moisture exiting the house or seeping around the edge of the casing during a rainstorm. The exterior of the casing and sash was primed at the factory. LEFT: Tom attaches the ½-inch jamb extensions to the side and top jambs with glue and brads. These slender strips of wood ensure that the surface of the jambs will be in the same plane as the wall surface.

The larger a vinyl window, the more it expands as temperatures change. That's why seals on this big window failed, but the small windows on either side are fog-free. Unfortunately, failed seals cannot be repaired; replacement is the only option.

When Tom installs a new window, his foremost goal is to make its perimeter watertight so it won't have to be replaced again. "I can't tell you how many times I've seen windows in relatively new houses completely rotted out," he says. To prevent that, he peeled off the old siding, protected the exposed sheathing with asphalt-impregnated kraft paper and stapled a waterproof, 9-inch-wide spline of fiberglass-reinforced polyethylene around the window opening. "It's the single most important step in the process," he says, because it keeps water from finding its way past the sheathing and into the framework. House-wrap alone won't do. "That's an air-infiltration barrier and does nothing to stop water," says Tom.

After stapling the splines, Tom slid the window, bottom edge first, into its opening. Once he

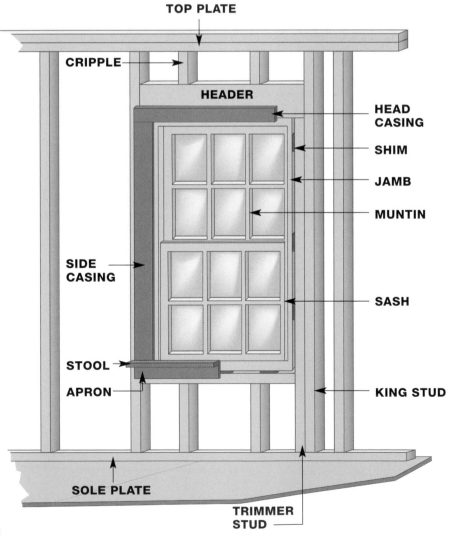

TOP PLATE

CRIPPLE

HEADER

HEAD CASING

SHIM

JAMB

MUNTIN

SIDE CASING

SASH

STOOL

APRON

KING STUD

SOLE PLATE

TRIMMER STUD

centered the unit, he tacked it in place through the casing with a 10d galvanized nail. Then he plumbed, leveled and checked its squareness by measuring both diagonals, just to make sure it hadn't racked during the installation. Tom's next job was to screw the window to the framing, then to caulk the narrow gap between the casing and the siding. After finishing the work outdoors, he moved inside to "trim out" the window.

He started by insulating the gap between the window frame and the wall framing. Overlooking that step can allow condensation to form inside the wall and wreak as much havoc as rainwater. Tom insulates and stops vapor in one step with canned, expanding polyurethane foam, a product he chooses and applies with care. "Put in too much and it can bow the jambs and make a window impossible to open," he says.

After the foam hardened, Tom trimmed it flush with the wall surface. That cleared the way for him to nail wood trim to the jambs and the trimmer stud (see drawing at left).

Overall, the work took about three hours to complete, but Tom won't have to repeat the effort anytime soon. "That first window lasted a couple hundred years," he says. "Let's hope this one lasts even longer."

FRAMING A NEW WINDOW

Replacing a window is one thing, but installing one where only wall existed before is a trickier proposition. The work can be hard, but the success of many kitchen remodeling projects hinges on adding new windows or moving old ones. Sometimes that lets you reposition a refrigerator, or maybe it turns a dark, blank wall into a sunny breakfast nook. In any case, says Tom, "It's preparation that makes the job come out right." In the case of a new window (or a new door, for that matter), he has to cut through the wall, remove studs, then install a header and support it. The header supports the weight once borne by the removed framing. All this calls for careful measurements, and it's generally a job best left to professionals. In part, that's because a pro can *usually* guess what lurks within the wall. "The last thing you want," says Tom, "is to slice through a wire or a water pipe. That's a good way to ruin your whole afternoon."

HOW TO ORDER A WINDOW

When Tom needs new windows to remodel old houses, he tries to find new that fits with the old. "You want to take all the steps to make sure they look original," says Tom.

At the show's project in Milton, Massachusetts, for example, the old windows each had a pair of sash, single-hung (only the lower one slid up and down) with a six-over-six arrangement (each sash had six panes of glass). For the sake of energy efficiency, however, Tom specified that the new double-hung windows must have insulated glass. To keep costs down, he asked for standard double-hung windows (two sliding sash), with applied wooden muntins, inside and out. "That approximated the look of the oldest windows," says Tom.

His window order also included the width and height of the rough opening (the hole formed by the header, rough sill and studs). By industry custom, the width is always listed before the height. These cannot be estimates. "Quite often, I've seen homeowners try to guess the size of the rough opening based on where they think the sill plate is, rather than taking off the trim to find out exactly," says Todd Dalen, of the architectural division of Marvin Windows. "And if you guess wrong, you end up with a window shorter than the one you're replacing." Properly sized, a new window won't have to be squeezed into the rough opening. Dalen says there should be a half-inch of space on the top and sides for proper shimming and insulation. The window should rest directly on the rough sill.

Finally, Tom made sure the replacement windows would have flat, primed exterior trim to match the originals. He could instead have ordered the windows with an exterior nailing flange (see center photo, right), and attached his own trim. "That's useful if you want more elaborate trim," he says. "But you'd have to make it yourself."

INSTALL IT RIGHT

A window won't last if it's surrounded by wet wood. Caulk on outside joints does not provide enough protection—it will eventually crack. So before he closes up a wall, Tom makes sure any water that gets in has an escape route. TOP: Tom seals the wall under the sill with a self-stick waterproofing strip that is usually used to prevent leaks on roofs. MIDDLE: If a window has nailing flanges—strips of aluminum that connect the window to the wall—Tom arranges them so that the top piece overlaps the side pieces. A window without flanges will include wood casing instead. BOTTOM: Tom plugs gaps around the window frame with low-expansion polyurethane foam, but goes easy on the trigger because too much foam could warp the frame.

Working With Doors

Consider adding a pocket door or reviving a hinged door

OPEN, SHUT, OPEN, SHUT—A DOOR IS SUCH A SIMPLE device, so easily taken for granted. Until, of course, it won't close, or it sticks . . . or it separates you from the kitchen of your dreams. An ill-placed opening sends traffic coursing through the work triangle of a kitchen rather than around it, encouraging conflict. Moving a door might resolve it.

Relocating a standard, hinged door involves the same sort of carpentry derring-do as moving a window (see page 147). But when considering the prospect, bear in mind that not all doors swing, and not all swinging doors swing well.

THE INS AND OUTS OF POCKET DOORS

Like a curtain separating for a stage performance, pocket doors roll apart to dramatically present the room beyond. Perhaps such theatrics explain the fashion of these disappearing doors in the Victorian era. Unlike doors that swing into the room, pocket doors simply roll sideways into cavities—or "pockets"—in the wall. This makes them great options anywhere that space is tight or use is infrequent, such as between a kitchen and a dining room.

The virtues of a pocket door, though, have always hung on its hardware. In the 19th century, builders' catalogs abounded with gizmos designed to effortlessly whisk the door out of sight. But even the best hardware of the times eventually broke or jammed under the strain of the heavy doors, which were then entombed inside their pockets or removed altogether.Until recently, poor hardware was the Achilles' heel of modern pocket doors, too, according to Tom Silva. But he adds that a new type of hardware, developed in Germany, has overcome these drawbacks. Its nylon-wheeled trucks, which glide smoothly and almost silently in a track of anodized aluminum, have a capacity of up to 352 pounds, enough to hold even the heaviest of doors.

The only prerequisite is that there be room for the pocket, a space equivalent to the door's width plus one-half inch, without any electrical wiring, ductwork, or plumbing in the way. Above the doorway, you'll need 4 to 6 inches of clearance for the hardware. Beyond these limitations, though, pocket doors will work for interior applications in almost any way imaginable. For a set of double doors, there's an optional pulley mechanism under the track that makes them move in unison when only one is being

TOP: A guide prevents the bottom of this pocket door from rattling.
ABOVE: Installing track for a new pocket-door in an old house requires access holes in the walls. Holes are easily patched, however.
RIGHT: A pocket door slips completely out of the way when it is not needed.

STRIPPING A DOOR

TOP: To reveal a door's original look, it can be stripped with a solvent-based liquid stripper that contains no acid, caustic chemicals, or methylene chloride. The door is immersed for six hours. Scouring pads are used to remove the first few coats of paint; a small brass brush (ABOVE) and a scraper remove the rest. LEFT: A new old door, sporting custom-blended red mahogany and cherry stain.

pushed or pulled. And special hardware even allows for curved units.

Neither the hardware nor the doors require special maintenance or care. In fact, having doors that virtually disappear makes housecleaning easier; you don't have to move them around to vacuum dust bunnies. "Pocket doors take a little more work to install," says Tom, "but if you need the space, they're worth it."

Finding a buried and long-abandoned pocket door during the course of kitchen remodeling is like finding buried treasure—unless you had planned to run plumbing in just that spot. "It happens all the time," says Rick Senk, a contractor with Beyer Construction in New Berlin, Wisconsin. "When the old wheels or track broke, people just shoved the

TUNING UP A HINGED DOOR

TOP OF DOOR STICKS: Drive a long screw through a sagging head jamb and into the door frame above it. Don't overdo it, though. It's easy to open a gap between the head and side casing or to split the jamb. You can also plane a bit off a door's head, but too many trims will make a door look out of proportion.

HINGES OUT OF ALIGNMENT OR UNEVEN VERTICAL REVEALS: Fit thin cardboard shims cut from cereal boxes into the jamb mortise beneath the hinges. Be careful, though. Too much shimming will cause the door to stick.

DOOR STICKS ON THE LATCH-SIDE JAMB: The problem may lie on the oppo-

doors into the pockets and closed up the jamb." Pocket doors were most common in houses built between about 1850 and 1910 that have a large opening between a living and dining room. The odds of finding a door increase if a wall is thicker than usual (say, 8 inches instead of 5 or 6 elsewhere in the house) and free of switches or outlets. "Look for drag marks on the floor and a molding or filler piece covering the center of the jamb," says Senk. The only way to know for sure, though, is to remove the casings and the jamb.

TIPS FOR REVIVING HINGED DOORS

If you're lucky, any existing hinged doors leading to your kitchen are in the right place. But the personality of an old door changes with the seasons. By August, heat often drives moisture deep into the grain, and the door swells and sticks.

TRIMMING A DOOR

RIGHT: One way to prevent splintering is to plane from the ends towards the middle. Another solution is to tack or clamp a piece of scrap wood to the door's edge. "When you reach the end of the wood with the plane, you're splitting the scrap instead of the door," Tom says.

LOWER RIGHT: Tom's door-trimming power plane has a right-angle shoe that makes the tool easy to steady as he slides it. "With any plane, you have to press down firmly," Tom says. "Otherwise, the nose will lift up, and you'll have an uneven cut."

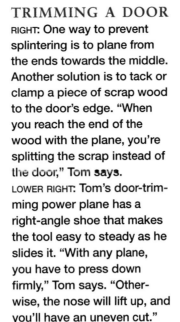

Period doorknobs can transform an otherwise dull door. Just be sure that the tube latch (ABOVE) will fit the knob's spindle (RIGHT).

site side, if the hinge leaves are loose or the hinge-side jamb is listing. Re-anchor loose leaves with longer hinge screws. Correct jamb tilt by driving a long screw behind the top hinge and into the door frame. If all else fails, shave a bit off the door stile with a block plane.

DOOR RESISTS BEING CLOSED: The door is hinge-bound. Shim the hinges, remount the hinge leaves on the jamb farther from the stop, or remove any hinge-side accretions of paint from the jamb, stop, and door edge.

MOISTURE TROUBLE: A door that functions well in the winter may swell into a nuisance with summer's humidity. Painting the top and bottom edges helps reduce seasonal swelling. Otherwise, trim the door with a block plane where needed.

Tom confronts a stubborn door with a jack plane and a little restraint. "You want to take off the minimum amount of wood necessary because the door is going to shrink again in the winter," says Tom. "If you remove too much, it will sit loose in the opening." His rule of thumb is that the reveal—the space between the door and jamb—should be ⅛ to 3/16 inch wide, or about the thickness of a nickel.

Examining one sticky bedroom door in his own house, Tom spends a little time getting a sense of its predicament. He opens and closes it to see where it catches, and he eyeballs the reveal. An uneven reveal may mean the hinges are loose or out of alignment. Then he makes any repairs. But after fixing them, if Tom finds that the door still sticks, humidity is the probable culprit. He pulls the hinge pins and removes the door for planing. As pine curls off the door's edge, Tom is well on his way to restoring the door's smooth swing.

Soldering Copper Pipes

Sooner or later, you'll either move kitchen supply pipes or repair them. Here's how

SINCE ITS INTRODUCTION IN THE 1920s, copper tubing has been the preferred material for distributing water within a home. Copper does not taint the water. It is accepted by all the building codes in the United States. It doesn't corrode (unless you have well water with an extraordinarily high level of sediments, acids or alkalis). And skilled plumbers are not the only ones who can join or repair it; homeowners can, too.

Brass and galvanized iron pipes, which preceded copper in residential plumbing, are joined by tricky threaded ends. The best way to join copper tubing, on the other hand, is by soldering, or sweating, the fittings together to form a metal-to-metal bond. Soldering is not difficult. Once you get the hang of it, it takes less than a minute to make a strong, leak-free joint that will last indefinitely. And it's a satisfying process. As one do-it-yourselfer described the work, "Learning to solder was the most liberating moment of my homeowning career."

Portable, reliable and cheap, a propane torch heats copper quickly. A torch with a self-igniting tip (RIGHT) keeps your fingers away from the flame when lighting up.

A shower faucet shows the complexity possible with soldered joints. Luckily, kitchen supply pipes aren't usually so involved.

THE SOLDER

Solder is a tin-based alloy that fuses with copper. Plumbers once used 50/50 solder—half tin, half lead; since 1986, the solder (and flux) used for drinking-water supply pipes in the United States must be lead-free. Look for solders combining tin and silver; avoid tin-antimony solder, which is harder to use. A UPC/IAPMO marking on the spool indicates that the solder has been tested and can be used in drinking-water systems.

Solder wire

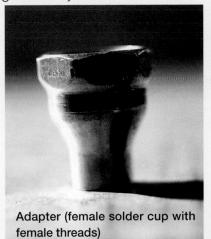

Adapter (female solder cup with female threads)

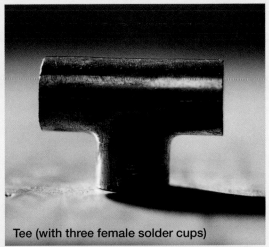

Tee (with three female solder cups)

Emery cloth ("scratch") and fitting brush

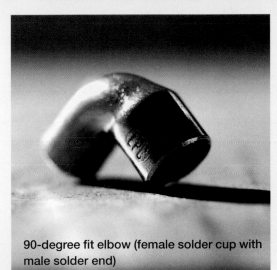

90-degree fit elbow (female solder cup with male solder end)

Tubing cutter

Fitting adapter (female solder cup with male thread)

Flux (soldering paste) and disposable acid brush

How to Solder

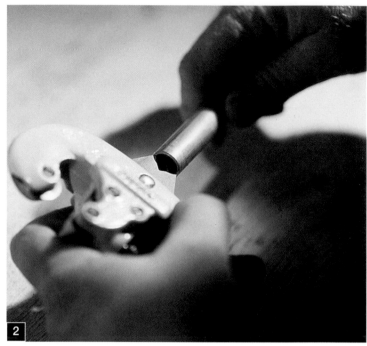

The secret to soldering is to have a clean joint with a perfecly round cross section. First, measure and mark a length of tube (1). Rotate a tubing cutter around the tube, tightening the handle slightly at each turn to avoid flatening the tube. Remove the burr inside with the triangular reamer (2) that folds out of the cutter; keep both edges of the reamer in contact with the tube so the tube stays round, and don't push too hard or the end will flare. Clean the end of the fitting with a fitting brush (3), turning it clockwise to avoid breaking the wire bristles. Use a brush the same diameter as the tubing; don't touch the surface afterward.

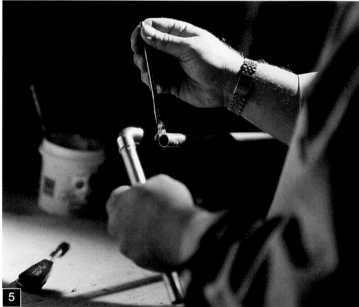

Polish the outside of the tube with fine-grit emery cloth (4). With a disposable acid brush, coat both mating surfaces with a thin layer of flux to neutralize oxides (5), then insert the tube into the fitting. Clean, flux, and fit all pieces together. Uncoil about 7 inches of solder wire; bend a 2-inch crook near the end. Holding a propane torch at an angle to the fitting, train the innerrmost blue flame on the fitting. When the flux bubbles, touch the tip of the solder wire to the side of the joint opposite the flame (6). (Never put flame on the solder itself.) When the solder liquefies and is sucked into the fitting, remove the flame and quickly run the tip of the solder around the joint until it is filled. Gently wipe the joint with a wet cloth to set the solder, then wait until all parts have cooled before testing.

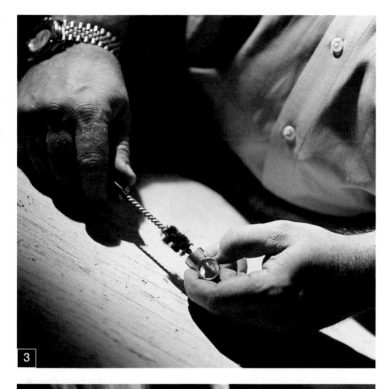

3

6

1. Protect nearby materials with a woven-fiber heat shield, available from plumbing-supply stores.

2. Water and hot solder don't mix. If the inside of the tube is wet, stuff a wad of white bread (no crust) into it. The bread absorbs drips while you're soldering, then dissolves when the water is turned on.

3. Flux is caustic: Don't get it on your skin or in your eyes. Wipe all residue off joints (it could corrode the copper); and flush plumbing thoroughly before drinking the water.

if it leaks, cut the tube a few inches from the leak, reheat the joint and remove the tube stub from the fitting. Be careful: It's hot. Using a straight coupling to bridge the cut, then clean, flux, and refit the tube (and fittings) as before, and resolder.

Installing Kitchen Cabinets

Careful attention to plumb and level will make your investment look great

WHEN TOM SILVA STARTED HIS CARPENTRY career more than 35 years ago, he often built the kitchen cabinets he installed for his customers. "Back then, it was still cost-effective for contractors to build them," he recalls. "Today, manufacturers assemble them faster and more economically than we can." They also offer a bewildering variety of styles and features, and you'll need time to sort through the options. That's hard enough, but the heavy lifting really begins soon after box after box of cabinets arrives at your house. Many people leave cabinet installation to the designer's crew, but it's a job you—and some helpers—can do.

As Tom explains it, the goal is to take the collection of cabinets and bring them together to make a beautiful piece of built-in furniture. The basic installation sequence is straightforward: You have to get everything straight, plumb, and level. But more often than not, the room itself lacks those attributes. "When walls aren't flat, floors aren't level, and corners aren't square, that's when it gets interesting," Tom says with a smile.

Cabinets hung the right way surmount such obstacles and become the solid centerpiece of a kitchen. "When you're done, you want the cabinets to look as though they were custom-made to fit the space," he says. That means tight joints, flush face frames, and perfectly aligned doors.

Before he screws the upper cabinets to the wall, Tom Silva sets them on a temporary, level wood cleat and shims them plumb. "If they're not positioned properly," he says, "the drawers won't fit and the doors won't open smoothly."

materials

Kitchen cabinets may look alike, Tom says, but "Durability depends on the bones—how a cabinet is constructed and what it's made of."

CARCASS: "I always look for a good, heavy box, one with a thick, solid back or rail that I can screw securely to the wall." Tom favors plywood (over particleboard or medium-density fiberboard), dadoed or mortised joints, and metal corner braces (A).

FINISHES: Catalyzed lacquers or conversion varnishes are the toughest; either can be applied over clear or painted wood.

FASTENERS: Screws are best, but unless you select custom-made units, most cabinets are held together with staples or brads.

DRAWERS: Dovetail joints (B) stand up to constant abuse better than simple box or butted joints. Fully extending drawer slides (C) cost more but allow complete access to the drawer interior.

HINGES: The exposed knuckles on leaf hinges befit a traditional look, but they are hard to adjust. Cup hinges (D), also known as European or concealed hinges, are more easily adjusted to keep doors hanging true.

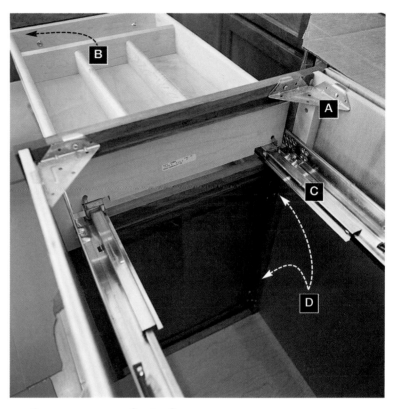

"Never assume that wall surfaces are flat, floors are level, or corners are square." —**Tom Silva**

TOOLS

1. Cordless drill: for securing cabinets to the wall and to each other
2. Bit set: for drilling holes and driving screws
3. Woodworking glue: for securing joints in trim
4. Angle finder (optional): for measuring the angle between adjacent walls
5. 4-in-1 screwdriver: for removing and securing door hardware quickly
6. Hammer: for nailing trim in place and driving shims
7. Trim saw (optional): for cutting shims flush
8. Chalk line: for snapping layout lines
9. Tape measure: for general measuring use
10. Folding rule: for measuring between surfaces that face each other
11. Bubble level: for determining level and plumb

12. Block plane: for back-beveling face frames and fine-tuning scribes
13. Compass: for scribing
14. Bar clamps: for holding cabinets together
15. Utility knife: for trimming shims.
16. 3/4-inch chisel: for shaving wood to tune fit
17. Framing square: for determining squareness of corners
18. Wood shims: for making cabinets plumb and level

ALSO NEEDED
6-foot stepladder: for reaching upper cabinets
Biscuit joiner (optional): for joining and aligning face frames
Hole saws: to cut holes for plumbing lines
Straightedge: for checking that face frames are flush

Installation

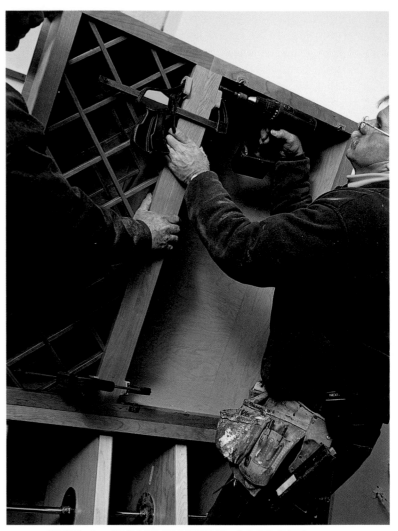

STEP 1: MARK THE LAYOUT LINES

- Mark a line on the wall about 48 inches off the floor (ABOVE). Using any sort of level (Tom used a laser level here), identify and mark additional reference points at the same height wherever the cabinets will be. Snap a chalk line to connect the marks, and measure from the chalk line down to the floor in several places. Mark the line where the measurement is the shortest; this is the high point of the floor.
- Directly beneath the mark for the high point, mark the height of your base cabinets, usually 34 inches above the floor. From that mark, extend a level layout line along the walls. The top of the base cabinets will be flush with this line.
- Measure 17 to 18 inches up from the base cabinet layout line, and snap a level chalk line for the bottom edge of the upper cabinets. Find the wall studs and mark every point where the center of a stud intersects both layout lines.
- Mark out the locations of all appliances.

TIP: If you have a tall cabinet for a pantry or built-in oven, it determines the height of the other upper cabinets.

STEP 2: JOIN THE UPPER CABINETS

- Remove doors, drawers, and movable shelves to make the cabinets lighter and easier to handle. Label everything with masking tape so each piece can be put back without mix-ups.
- Position a straight 1x3 cleat just beneath the layout line for the upper cabinets. Drive 2-inch drywall screws through this temporary cleat into every other stud.
- With the cabinets resting on the floor, align the face frame of the upper corner cabinet so it is flush with the frame of the neighboring cabinet. Clamp the two together. Verify that the face frames are still flush with one another by holding a straightedge against the joint.
- Drill counterbored pilot holes (see Glossary, page 162) through the edge of one face frame and into the other face frame, top and bottom. Drive 2-inch screws into these holes to hold the cabinets tightly together (ABOVE).

TIP: "You don't want any gaps showing where face frames join," Tom says. "That's a sign of poor workmanship."

STEP 3: HANG THE UPPER CABINETS

- With one or two helpers, lift the corner cabinet assembly into place and rest it on the cleat (ABOVE).
- As a helper steadies the assembly, check the cabinet face with a level to see if it's plumb. If it is, drive four 2½-inch deck screws (with washers) through the back of the cabinet, top and bottom, and into the studs. (Don't use drywall screws—they can snap when used this way.) If the face is *not* plumb, slip shims between the cabinet back and the wall at the stud locations. (To shim out the bottom, support the cabinet and remove the cleat.) When the cabinet is plumb, screw it to the studs through the shims.
- Lift the remaining cabinets onto the cleat, align their faces flush with those already installed, and clamp and screw the edges together (see Step 2). Shim cabinets as necessary, then fasten them with deck screws and washers as above.
- Close any gap between the wall and the end cabinet by scribing its stile or back edge (see Glossary), or by covering the gap with trim.

STEP 4: INSTALL THE CORNER BASE CABINET

- Jockey the corner cabinet into position. Shim it up from the floor (ABOVE) until its back edge meets the layout line.
- Where plumbing pipes stick out from the surface of the wall, push the shimmed cabinet against them and mark their locations on its back panel. Turn the cabinet around and drill holes through the back with an appropriate-size hole saw. Reposition the cabinet.
- Using a level, check the face of the cabinet for plumb. If it's not plumb, insert shims between the floor and the bottom of the cabinet, or between the wall and the back of the cabinet, at the stud locations.
- Check that the top of the cabinet is level, and add shims underneath as necessary.
- With the cabinet against its shims, drive deck screws (with washers) through the cabinet back and into the studs (BELOW). At the shims, counterbore and fasten the cabinet to the floor with deck screws (without washers).

STEP 5: INSTALL REMAINING BASE CABINETS

- Working out from the installed corner cabinet, shim the adjacent cabinets out from the wall (at the stud locations) and up from the floor so that the face frames are plumb and the tops are level and even with the layout line.
- Align each cabinet so its face is flush with its already-installed neighbor. Clamp them together, counterbore through the edge of the face frames, and fasten them together with 2-inch screws.
- At the shims, drive the deck screws (with washers) through the cabinet back and into studs as before.
- Close any gap between the wall and the end cabinet by scribing its stile or the back edge of its side panel. Or, cover the gap with trim.
- Using a utility knife, score any shims that protrude beyond the edges of the cabinets, then snap off their ends.
- Remove all the upper-cabinet support cleats and fill the screw holes with spackle.
- Reinstall the drawers and shelves in their original cabinets.

STEP 6: REPLACE DOORS, INSTALL TOEKICK

- Reinstall the cabinet doors (LEFT). For overlay doors, which cover the cabinet frame, adjust the hinges so that the doors hang straight. For an inset door, adjust the hinges so the door is flush with the face frame and shows a uniform reveal (gap) around its perimeter.
- Using 1-inch brads, fasten the toekick trim to the base cabinets. Fit the longest pieces first, then cut and install the shorter pieces. Close any gaps between the floor and trim by scribing the trim, or cover them by brad-nailing a shoe molding to the floor. Recess the nail heads with a nailset and cover them with wood putty or color-matched wax stick.
- If you're using crown molding to trim out the upper cabinets, align the molding's bottom edge with a level layout line marked above the tops of the doors. Fasten the molding to the cabinet with 1- to 2-inch finish nails. Glue the molding's end joints. Recess the nailheads with a nail set and cover them with wood putty or color-matched wax stick.

GLOSSARY: **BACK BEVEL:** A 2- to 5-degree angle planed along the edge of a cabinet or a piece of trim, where it will butt another object. This makes a tight fit on the joint's visible surface. The bevel always slants away from (and does not touch) the exposed face of the piece being planed. **COUNTERBORE:** A bit that simultaneously drills a pilot hole and cuts a recess for the screwhead so it can be covered with a plug or wood putty. **SCRIBE:** A cut made in a cabinet or trim piece that follows the contour of an adjoining surface.

fit to be tight

Cabinets are made straight and square, but the walls and floors they rest against are rarely so. That's where shims come in handy. When tapped into place by just the right amount, these wedge-shaped pieces of wood can plumb and level a cabinet, despite a room's irregularities.

But when walls meet at an angle greater than 90 degrees, shims alone may not be the answer; they can cause the cabinets to project out too far, leaving an unsightly gap at the ends. "Corner cabinets are usually the first ones to be installed," Tom Silva explains, "so if they don't fit right, the rest of the cabinets probably won't, either." His solution is to remove some drywall so the backs of the corner cabinets (both upper and base) nestle closer to the studs.

Finally, if the walls aren't straight where a bank of cabinets ends, the best way to hide the gap, in Tom's view, is to scribe a tight fit. After the cabinet is plumbed and leveled, he cuts its stile (if the cabinet butts a wall) or the back edge of its side panel so that it follows exactly the irregular contours of the wall. Before scribing, Tom always back-bevels the edge with a block plane (right). Back-beveling narrows the edge so the scribe can be fine-tuned faster and more easily.

cabinet anatomy & installation details

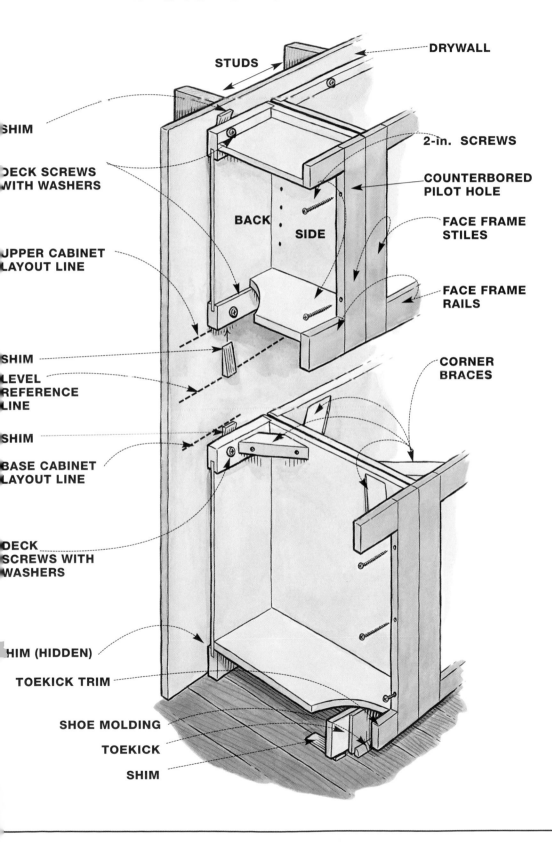

STUDS

DRYWALL

SHIM

DECK SCREWS WITH WASHERS

2-in. SCREWS

COUNTERBORED PILOT HOLE

BACK

SIDE

FACE FRAME STILES

UPPER CABINET LAYOUT LINE

SHIM

FACE FRAME RAILS

LEVEL REFERENCE LINE

SHIM

CORNER BRACES

BASE CABINET LAYOUT LINE

DECK SCREWS WITH WASHERS

SHIM (HIDDEN)

TOEKICK TRIM

SHOE MOLDING

TOEKICK

SHIM

PLANNING TIPS

• Lay a wood floor before hanging cabinets. "It goes down a whole lot faster in an empty room," says Tom Sil-va. Protect it with thick mover's pads during cabinet installation. Sheet flooring is more easily damaged, so lay it after the cabinets are in.

• Using a 4-foot level, a framing square, and a straight 2x4, check the walls and corners to see if they are plumb, square, and straight. Dips, bubbles, or angles may require scribe-fitting, shimming, or other alterations of the wall.

• Install electrical lines for the range, dishwasher, garbage disposer, refrigerator, and vent hood. Install receptacles above your countertop backsplash according to local code. Also, rough in the wiring for cabinet lights and their wall-mounted switches.

• Rough in supply and drain lines before installing any of the cabinets.

Tiling A Floor

The basic techniques for sticking tile to a floor also work on other kitchen tile projects

JOE FERRANTE HAS BEEN LAYING TILE FOR MORE THAN 30 years—a good number of them for *This Old House* contractor Tom Silva—and after all this time, he's still enamored of the material. "I love tile," he says. "It's beautiful, it's durable, and it doesn't require much maintenance."

On a floor, tiles call for careful installation or they won't survive parading feet and the vast array of spills dished out in a kitchen, where floors go from bone dry to sopping wet faster than you can say "puddle." But if you can tile a floor with success, almost any kitchen tiling job is open to you, including walls and countertops.

"Anytime I approach a new job, I make sure the area about to be tiled—that's called the substrate—is stiff enough so it won't flex," says Ferrante. Preparing the substrate and using the proper tile-setting materials are critical. Add some basic tools and some basic, time-tested techniques, and any kitchen tile work will last a lifetime.

A glass inset tile is about to find its home in a field of ceramic. Tiling contractor Joe Ferrante normally just lays floor tiles in a bed of thinset, a cement-based adhesive, but he always butters it on the backs of glass tiles to ensure even coverage on the translucent material. Uneven coverage will be visible for the life of the tile floor.

materials

Ask Joe Ferrante what the best surface is for setting tile, and he'll answer without hesitation: "A mud job." The centuries-old technique for making a tiling base, also known as a mortar bed, uses nothing more than a stiff mix of portland cement, sand, and water, reinforced with steel mesh. When trowel-packed to a minimum ¾-inch thickness, the surface becomes smooth, hard, flat, and immune to water: a perfect complement to brittle ceramics. No other substrate can compare in longevity—examples still survive from Roman times—but the skill and time required to mix and trowel it flat make a mud job the most expensive option.

Cement-based manufactured substrates—backerboard—are thinner and can be installed by almost anyone. But because they are a uniform thickness, they follow humps and hollows in the subfloor, making it difficult to achieve a perfectly flat surface. One substance that Ferrante refuses to tile directly over is plywood. "It moves too much and cracks the tile and the grout," he says. "Most of the jobs I'm called in to fix are set directly on plywood."

A. SITE-MIXED MORTAR BED reinforced with galvanized steel mesh is the substrate favored by skilled tilers.

B. FIBERGLASS-REINFORCED CEMENT backerboard (shown here with thinset) comes in ½-inch-thick panels.

C. FIBER-CEMENT backerboard—autoclaved portland cement set with cellulose—is also ½ inch thick.

D. MORTAR TROWELED into ½-inch-thick nylon mesh requires less skill than a mortar bed.

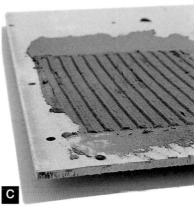

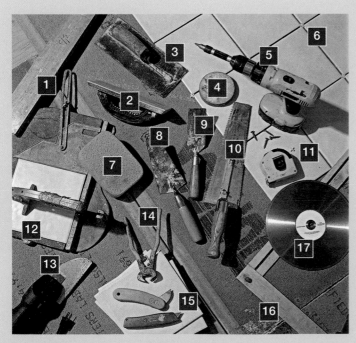

TOOLS

1. **10-foot straightedge:** for aligning rows of tile
2. **Rubber float:** for spreading grout
3. **Notched trowel:** for spreading adhesive (notch size should be the same as the thickness of the tile)
4. **Rubbing stone:** for smoothing cut tile edges
5. **Cordless drill and epoxy-coated screws:** for securing cement backerboard to the subfloor
6. **Tile spacers:** to ensure consistent joints
7. **Foam sponge:** for wiping up grout haze
8. **Mason's trowel:** for mixing thinset and grout
9. **Margin trowel:** for cleaning cured joint lines and applying waterproof membranes to joints
10. **Flush-cut saw:** for undercutting wood trim
11. **Tape measure:** for general measuring work
12. **Snap cutter:** quickly cuts tile in one stroke
13. **Power flush-cut saw:** a professional's choice for undercutting wood trim
14. **Nibblers:** for breaking small pieces off a tile to shape it
15. **Carbide-tipped scorer and a utility knife:** for cutting backerboard
16. **Folding layout square:** for checking squareness
17. **Diamond blade:** used with a wetsaw for quick, smooth cuts on tile

Installation

STEP 1: LAYOUT ROOM

- Find the midpoint of each wall and snap a chalk line on the floor between opposite points. The lines crossing at the center of the room mark the starting point for figuring layout.
- Off to one side, dry-lay tiles in a row extending more than half the length of the room. Space them evenly, about ³⁄₁₆ to ¼ inch apart, along a straightedge. For consistent joint width, use tile spacers. This dry-laid row will help to fine-tune the layout and determine the size of cut tiles.
- At the center of the room, place a tile so its corner is at the point where the chalk lines cross and two edges touch the lines. Measure the distance from one wall (call it A) to the nearest edge of the tile. Now, go to the tile row and, starting at a joint, measure along the row and mark the distance you just came up with (LEFT). The mark shows the width of the tile that will touch the wall. If that width is less than 2 inches, go back to the center tile (the one at the chalk lines). Move it along the chalk line perpendicular to and away from wall A—this will give you a wider cut tile.
- From the center tile, measure as before to the wall opposite A (call it B) and again mark this distance along the tile row. Adjust the center tile along the A-to-B chalk line until measurements to walls A and B show that the size of the pieces that will fit against each wall are roughly the same.
- Once you've made the final adjustment along the A-to-B line, mark the center tile where it touches the chalk line between the other two walls (call them C and D). Keep these marks aligned with the C-to-D chalk line, and repeat the same measuring and adjusting process that you used before (for walls A and B) between walls C and D.
- Once you're satisfied with the position of the center tile, lay a straightedge parallel with the C-to-D chalk line and against one side of this tile. Mark the straightedge where it meets a corner of the tile. This mark is your starting point for laying tile. Don't to move the straightedge until the first row of tile is set.
- Trim door casings with a flush-cut saw so tile can slip beneath. Cut with saw held flat against a tile on top of a piece of cardboard (to represent the thickness of the thinset). Don't cut into the wall or door jamb.

STEP 4: CUT TILES

- Make straight cuts with a snap cutter. When the waste piece is more than an inch wide, score the tile with one firm stroke, then break it by pushing down on the handle. Smooth cut edges with a rubbing stone. If the waste is less than an inch wide, score the tile and snap pieces off with nibblers. Or cut the tile with a wet saw.
- To fit a tile around an outside corner, hold one edge against the wall and mark the tile where it touches the corner. Pencil a line all the way across the tile. Then, without turning the tile, move it to the other side of the corner and again mark where tile and corner meet (RIGHT). Mark an X on the part to be cut away.
- On a wet saw (INSET), cut the tile from the mark to the line, taking care not to go beyond the line. Then turn the tile and cut along the line next to the X, up to but not beyond the first cut. As you near the end of the cut, lift up the tile edge farthest from you to help free the waste.
- For curved or scribed cuts, make parallel slices with the wet saw into the waste section, up to but not past the line marking the cut. Then break away the remaining "fingers" with nibblers.

STEP 2: SPREAD ADHESIVE

- Chuck a mixer attachment into a drill and blend the powdered thinset with latex additive—not water—until it's the consistency of mayonnaise. Slake (let it rest) for 5 to 10 minutes. Mix only as much thinset as you can use in about two hours. After that, it becomes too firm to be troweled.
- With the flat edge of a trowel, spread a thin layer of thinset (the scratch coat) over a 2-by-3-foot area next to the straightedge.
- Before the scratch coat dries, apply more thinset using the notched edge of the trowel. Hold the trowel at a 45-degree angle to the floor and spread the thinset evenly in broad curved strokes, then finish with a straight pass (ABOVE), which ensures the best adhesion. Combing the thinset into furrows like this allows air to escape as the tile is set.

TIP: When spreading thinset, press down hard so that the trowel makes a scraping sound.

STEP 3: SET THE TILE

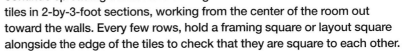

- Gently lay a tile on thinset next to the straightedge. With fingertips spread wide, push down with a slight twist of the wrist (RIGHT).
- Use this same technique to set each tile, making one row along the straightedge. Use tile spacers to ensure even joints.
- Move the straightedge out of the way and lay the next row alongside the first, using the edge of the tile as your guide. Then continue spreading thinset and setting tiles in 2-by-3-foot sections, working from the center of the room out toward the walls. Every few rows, hold a framing square or layout square alongside the edge of the tiles to check that they are square to each other.

TIP: Consistent finger pressure (and plenty of practice) helps to prevent lippage—the condition where a tile's edge is higher or lower than its neighbors.

installing backerboard

If a budget doesn't allow for an old-fashioned mud job, or if a doorway can't accommodate the mortar's added thickness, Ferrante installs backerboard, ½-inch-thick panels of cement mortar sandwiched between of sheets of fiberglass scrim. First he spreads a layer of construction adhesive or thinset over the subfloor (ABOVE) with a $\frac{5}{32}$-inch notched trowel, lays the 3-by-5-foot panels perpendicular to the joists, and screws the panels to the floor, driving epoxy-covered backerboard

screws every 8 inches over the panel's surface. "You want them long enough to penetrate the subfloor but not go through it," he says. "Longer screws might hit some plumbing, and that's not a good thing." To reduce the chances of the tile cracking along the joints in the backerboard, he staggers the panels and trowels a gummy antifracture membrane over all the joints (RIGHT). Once the membrane cures, the floor is ready for thinset and tile.

STEP 5: GROUT

- After tile sets for 24 at least hours, use a margin trowel to scrape off any thinset on the tile surface or in the joints.
- Mix up a batch of grout to a looser-than-mayonnaise consistency. Add water a little at a time by squeezing it from a sponge.
- Scoop a trowelful of grout onto the floor and spread it with a float held at a 45-degree angle to the floor (TOP LEFT). Push grout into the joints by first moving the float in line with the joints, then diagonal to them. Work from the edges of the room toward the center.
- The grout should be firm to the touch before washing. Wipe away haze with a barely damp, well-squeezed sponge rinsed often in a bucket of water.
- Again, wait for the grout to haze over, then wipe tiles with a sponge. Repeat until tile is clean (BOTTOM LEFT).

TIP: Don't be too aggressive when wiping up grout haze, or you could pull grout out of the joints.

Laying Engineered Wood Floors

Manufactured for stability, this wood can make it in the kitchen

JEFF HOSKING, A HARDWOOD FLOORING CONSULTANT FOR *This Old House*, began laying floors about 35 years ago, as an apprentice to his father. Back then, 90 percent of his work was installing long, solid strips of wood, fastened with nails. But now, about half of the flooring Hosking puts down is engineered—made of thin sheets of wood glued together like plywood.

Solid wood is classic and can last a century, but engineered flooring, which comes with a factory-applied finish, offers a quicker, easier, and less messy way to get a new floor. And because the product is laminated, it's more stable than solid wood, so you can put it over concrete or radiant floors, in a basement or a kitchen, and not worry much about shrinkage or warping. And, Hosking says, the finishes are far more durable than anything he can apply on site. Still, buyers must be aware that the quality of this flooring varies considerably: Obtaining and comparing samples is an important first step of the installation process.

For top-of-the-line engineered strips, a homeowner will pay $8 to $11 per square foot. That's higher than solid-wood planks, but homeowners can offset the expense by tackling the installation themselves. "It's far easier than sanding and finishing a traditional floor," Hosking says. He tells his do-it-yourself customers to call him if they have any trouble, but 95 percent manage without a hitch. His advice: "Just take it slow."

Jeff Hosking sinks a staple into a strip of engineered wood flooring just ⁵⁄₁₆ inch thick. To speed the installation, he racks up several courses of loose strips in front of him, their end joints already fitted and randomly staggered. He then works diagonally across the room.

materials

There are considerable differences in the way engineered wood flooring is made, and that can affect its appearance and durability. Here's what to look for before buying. **WEAR LAYER THICKNESS:** "The life of a floor is measured above the tongue," says Hosking. In engineered flooring, this is known as the wear layer. A ⅛-inch wear layer, for instance, can survive only about three refinishings. A ³⁄₁₆-inch layer, by contrast, can be sanded five times, almost as many times as a solid-wood floor. The life of a wear layer also depends on the hardness of the wood used (the harder the better) and how it is milled: A quarter-sawn layer is more stable and wear-resistant than one that's flat-sawn. **NUMBER OF LAYERS:** "More layers of wood means more stability," says Hosking, and a more stable floor is less likely to warp or have joints open up. **OVERWOOD:** This noticeable variation in the thickness of adjacent strips is a sign of poor quality control. To find it, butt several samples side to side and end to end on a flat surface. **EDGES:** On some floors, a slight bevel milled along the top edge disguises over-wood and masks minor irregularities in the subfloor, but results in visible grooves between adjacent strips. Square-edged flooring has a smoother look but may telegraph any irregularities in the subfloor. **FINISH:** Compare the number of coats and the details of the finish warranty, and inspect samples for sheen and smoothness.

"You save so much more money by laying flooring yourself that you can easily afford to rent the right tools" —**Jeff Hosking**

TOOLS

1. 8-foot straightedge: for checking flatness of subfloor

2. Fine-tooth handsaw: for trimming door casing

3. Pneumatic brad nailer: for fastening the first courses of flooring (alternative: hammer and nailset)

4. Miter saw (with carbide blade): for cutting flooring strips to length (alternative: backsaw with miter box)

5. Jigsaw: for trimming pieces to fit around vents and other obstacles (alternative: coping saw)

6. Pneumatic staple gun: for securing flooring to subfloor (alternative: manual hammer stapler)

7. Notched trowel: for spreading adhesive for glue-down installations

8. Plaster trowel: for spreading filler to level an uneven subfloor

9. Combination square: for marking cut lines

10. Utility knife: for cutting felt and general trimming

11. Rubber mallet: for tapping floor boards together

12. Pull bar: for snugging together strips close to wall (alternative: pry bar)

13. Plastic tapping block: for nudging a strip tightly to its neighbor without damaging the fragile tongue

14. Hammer: used with tapping block to snug up flooring, and with nailset to set finish nails

15. Hammer tacker: for securing builder's felt to floor

16. Tape measure: for taking measurements

17. Masking tape: for holding together glued-down boards until the adhesive has time to set

18. Cordless drill (with spade bit): for notching flooring around baseboard heating pipes

ALSO NEEDED

Air compressor: for powering pneumatic tools. A 4.5-gallon, 1.5-hp model was used for this project

Table saw: for cutting the last row of flooring to width

STEP 1: LEVEL THE SUBFLOOR

- With a pry bar, gently remove the baseboard trim. Also remove the end caps on baseboard heaters, the registers for forced-air vents, the plates for floor receptacles, and any other obstructions. Add a box extender to the floor receptacles, if required by local electrical code.
- Walk over every inch of the area and listen for squeaks. Wherever the existing wood flooring is loose, batten it down with ringshank nails or Phillips-head screws, and set them flush. Fasteners should penetrate at least ¾ inch into the floor framing. Repair loose or damaged sheet flooring. Over badly damaged floors, glue and fasten sheets of AC-grade ¼-inch plywood, with the "A" side (the better side) facing up.
- Check for flatness by sweeping a 10-foot straightedge across the floor. Mark the floor wherever light shows underneath the edge. Level humps with a belt sander. Fill depressions deeper than ⅛ inch with troweled-on patching compound (ABOVE); sand it smooth when dry.

STEP 2: FINAL PREP

- Trim off (undercut) the bottoms of door casings using a handsaw lying flat on a scrap of the new flooring (ABOVE).
- Vacuum the entire floor to clean up all dust, wood scraps, and debris.
- Cover the subfloor with 15-pound builder's felt and run it in the same direction as the new flooring (in line with the longest walls, typically). Butt the felt's edges together and use a hammer tacker to staple down each edge every 4 feet or so. Trim felt to within ½ inch of walls.
- After the floor is covered, drive any poorly set staples flush.

TIP: Cut openings in the felt with a utility knife each time you encounter a vent or outlet. You're likely to forget where they are if you wait until the whole floor is felted.

STEP 4: TOENAIL

- Once the first course is in place, drive 1½ inch brads at a 45-degree angle through the strip's tongue and into the subfloor, a technique called toe-nailing (LEFT). Repeat every 4 inches. Don't nail any closer than 2 inches from the end of the strip.
- Slip the second course of flooring over the tongues of the first and snug up the strips with a mallet or a tapping block and hammer. As you go, offset end joints by at least 12 inches from those in the first course. Toenail them with the brad nailer as before, but don't facenail.
- Because there are tongues and grooves milled into the ends of this flooring, the ends shouldn't be cut, except when they meet a wall or obstruction.

TIP: Choose each piece of flooring for length rather than color or grain. "The farther apart the end joints on neighboring courses are, the better the floor will look," says Hosking.

STEP 3: SET THE STARTER COURSE

- Start laying the floor in a corner, along the longest exterior wall, which is more likely than a partition wall to be straight and square.
- Place ½-inch-thick wood spacers against the starting wall and adjacent wall. This makes an expansion gap that prevents buckling. Butt the grooves (not the tongues) of a long strip of flooring against them.
- With a mallet, snug together the ends of more long strips. At the end of the course, fit a strip (no shorter than 10 inches) ½ inch from wall.
- When the first course is set, place a straightedge beside the tongues. Carefully move the flooring in or out until all the tongues line up precisely with that edge and all the end joints are good and tight.
- Using a brad nailer loaded with 1½-inch brads, facenail each board every 8 inches and within 1 inch of the wall (LEFT). Adjust the nailer to set the brads slightly below the floor surface. Check tongue alignment as you go.

STEP 5: STAPLE THE FLOOR

- Tap the next course snugly into place with hammer and block (LEFT). If this course is too close to the wall to use a pneumatic staple gun, toenail it.
- Lay out the next five courses on the floor and fit the ends together. The goal of this process, called racking, is to stagger the end joints randomly across the floor's field. Offset the end joints in adjacent courses at least 12 inches, and the joints of every third course at least one inch.
- Staple the remaining flooring through its tongues using the staple gun (ABOVE). This tool shoots 1-inch narrow-crown staples, which hold better than nails of the same size. A shoe holds it at a 45-degree angle. Fire staples every 4 to 5 inches, and no closer than 2 inches from an end.
- Continue racking, tapping, and stapling until you reach the wall opposite your starting point.

TIP: As you rack the flooring, check each piece for imperfections, particularly at edges and ends. Set flawed pieces aside to use as cutting stock. Discard any that are warped or bowed.

STEP 6: FINAL FITTING

• With a jigsaw, cut flooring around ducts and outlets as you encounter them. Always cover exposed edges with mitered trim pieces, which come from the manufacturer already finished. Fasten trim in place with a brad nailer.

• When you reach the wall opposite the starting wall, and the stapler can no longer be used, toenail the next-to-last courses with the brad nailer.

• Using a table saw, cut off the tongue side of the strips for the last course. Be sure to leave a ½-inch expansion space between this final course and the wall.

• Slip the strips into place and force them tightly against the previous course with a pull bar or pry bar (LEFT). Facenail them with the brad nailer.

• Vacuum the floor, then fill all facenail holes with colored putty blended to match the wood. Wipe off the excess with a cloth.

• Remove all spacers and install the baseboard and paint as needed. Put felt pads on the bottom of furniture and chair legs to protect the finish from scratches. Finally, take a walk on your new floor (RIGHT).

wood over concrete? no problem

Because engineered flooring is so thin and dimensionally stable, it can also be glued either directly to a subfloor or one piece to another. By dispensing with nails and staples, such methods allow a wood floor to go directly over concrete, something rarely advisable with solid wood. Planks that are 5 inches wide or more can be glued down or, in some cases, left to "float" over a vapor barrier. Narrow strips have to be glued down.

GLUED-DOWN FLOOR. Working like a tilesetter, Hosking spreads a gooey urethane adhesive over the concrete with a No. 9 notched trowel and sticks the flooring into it, piece by piece (right). Once the adhesive cures, in about one or two days, the floor is ready to use. The keys to success here are controlling moisture and using a dependable adhesive. A newly poured concrete slab should cure at least 30 days—"Longer is better," says Hosking—and existing floors must be tested (by taping down a patch of foil) to be sure water vapor isn't moving through them. He admits that gluing floors down is messier than nailing them. "And you have to work fast, or the adhesive will skin over and the flooring won't stick," Hosking explains.

FLOATING FLOOR. With this technique, the planks are glued only to each other, edge-to-edge, using an aliphatic resin glue recommended by the manufacturer. The finished floor becomes, in effect, one large panel, so joints stay tight. A thin sheet of closed-cell foam under the floor allows it to contract and expand as a unit. The foam also provides cushioning, offers a small measure of thermal and acoustic insulation, and serves as a vapor barrier, all features suited to installations over concrete.

glued-down flooring

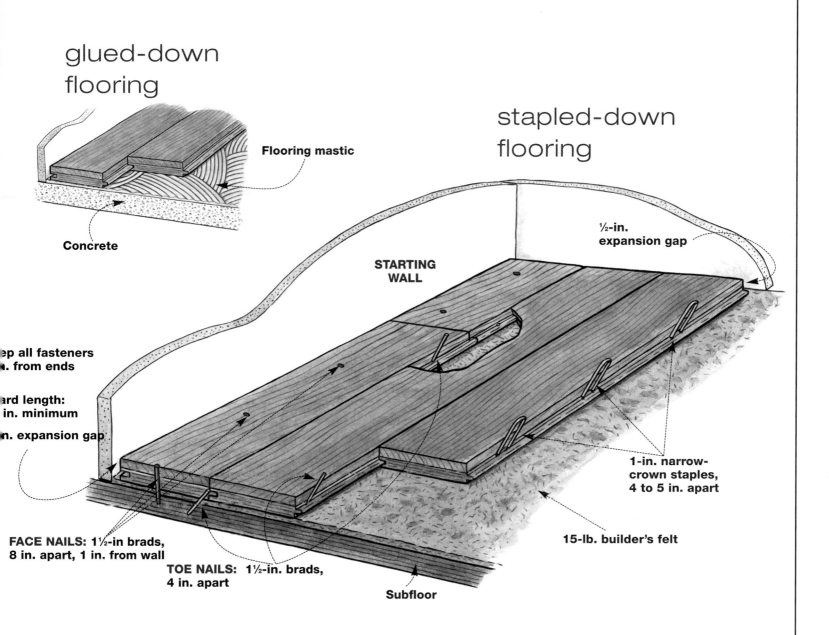

Flooring mastic

Concrete

stapled-down flooring

½-in. expansion gap

STARTING WALL

ep all fasteners
. from ends

rd length:
in. minimum

n. expansion gap

FACE NAILS: 1½-in brads,
8 in. apart, 1 in. from wall

TOE NAILS: 1½-in. brads,
4 in. apart

Subfloor

1-in. narrow-
crown staples,
4 to 5 in. apart

15-lb. builder's felt

PLANNING AHEAD

• To estimate how much flooring to buy, calculate the square footage and add a waste allowance: 5 to 7 percent for straight-course floors; 15 percent for a herringbone pattern. For metric materials, 1 square meter equals about 10½ square feet.

• Take an inventory of all edges that won't be covered by baseboard, including hearths, stairs, and cabinets. Order enough factory-finished trim to cover these edges.

• Let flooring acclimate in open boxes for 3 to 4 days in the room where it will be laid. Wait at least a week before opening boxes in rooms where drywall or plaster has just been installed. Don't store flooring in a basement or garage, or any other location where it might absorb moisture.

• "Try to run the flooring parallel to the longest wall in a room," says Hosking. "It makes the space seem bigger." This also reduces the amount of cutting that's required.

AUTHORS: Max Alexander, Meghan Anderson, Thomas Baker, John Banta, Akiko Busch, Joe Carter, Joseph D'Agnese, Bettie Dixon, Paul Engstrom, Mark Feirer, Thomas Fields-Meyers, Barbara Flanagan, Douglas Gatenbein, Dianne Harris, Anna Holbrook, Jeanne Huber, Jill Kirchner, Anne Krueger, Brad Lemley, Betty Ming Lui, Jack McClintock, Rhoda Murphy, Romy Pokorny, Hope Reeves, John Rhia, Curtis Rist, Victoria Rowan, Cynthia Sanz, May Kelly Selover, Tim Snyder, Wendy Talarico, Michael Wagner

PHOTOGRAPHERS: Eric Axene, Timothy Bell, John Blais, Pascal Blancon, Kay Boecker, Dan Borris, Fran Brennan, Burazin Photography, David Carmack, Kindra Clineff, Four Legs Photography, Michael Grimm, John Gruen, Darrin Haddad, Eric Heimlich/Steve Hinds Photography, Todd Hido, Chad Holder, Keller & Keller, Kubani, Nedjeljko Matura, Shelley Metcalf, Josha McHugh, Garry McLeod, Benjamin Oliver, Greg Premru, Craig Raine, Erik Rank, Eric Roth, Kolin Smith, Danny Turner, Cheryl Ungar, Joe Yutkins

ILLUSTRATORS: Michael Freeman, Homer Jolly, Greg Nemec